UNDER THE RUBBLE

AND OTHER STORIES

BARB LATAILLADE

the Peppertree Press
Sarasota, Florida

For information regarding permission,
call 941-922-2662 or contact us at our website:
www.peppertreepublishing.com or write to:
the Peppertree Press, LLC.
Attention: Publisher
1269 First Street, Suite 7
Sarasota, Florida 34236

ISBN: 978-1-936343-59-1

Library of Congress Number: 2010942319

Printed in the U.S.A.

Printed December 2010

ACKNOWLEDGMENTS

Thanks to my artist and editors who have labored with me until the completion of this book. You have taught me so much, and I have felt your encouragement and commitment in this work.

EDITORS:
Martha DiPalma
Ann Witkower
Kay Harper

ARTIST:
Rob Woodrum

Our home and mission house before the quake

FROM MY HEART TO YOURS

Barbara is a common name among Americans, but perhaps few know its meaning, "wanderer and foreigner." My parents had no idea how my name would be lived out in reality. Although as Christians, we are all pilgrims and foreigners on this earth, a few of us have the privilege of being a pilgrim in a foreign country as well.

I was born in Illinois in an Amish family, the second of six children. My parents were strong Christians. The Bible was the foundation of our family. At thirteen, I gave my life to the Lord and was baptized.

When I was twenty-one I traveled to northern Ontario, Canada, and worked among the Indians for a summer. This was an enriching experience and my first mission effort. Missionary work ran "thick in my blood." It just wouldn't go away.

At 28, I moved to Florida. God led me in various steps toward a lifetime of mission work. Always thinking I would return to the Indians in Canada, I never dreamed God had plans for me to go further south. Because the church I was attending had a work in Haiti, I became involved in their mission.

After I had been in Haiti for several years I met Patrick, a native of Haiti, who is now my husband. We have two children who were raised in Haiti, but now live in the states. In addition we have three beautiful grandchildren.

At the writing of this book, I have served in Haiti for twenty-nine years. Its stories are not only my experiences, but also some of my husband's and of a few natives we have met over the years in Haiti.

These stories will provide a bird's-eye view of a cross-cultural life. My prayer is that you will be blessed, and see God's hand among His people in Haiti.

The stories are true, however some names have been changed to protect those involved.

FACTS ABOUT HAITI

In 1492, Christopher Columbus arrived on the Island of Hispaniola, which is shared by Haiti and the Dominican Republic. Haiti was lush with fruits and mahogany trees, as well as gold and other precious stones. It was given the title "Pearl of the Caribbean" by the French during the years when they ruled the island.

Location: Haiti is in the Caribbean Sea, a part of the Antilles Islands. It is 800 miles south of Miami, Florida. Port au Prince is its capital.

Economy and Politics: Political violence, harsh dictatorship, depletion of natural resources and overwhelming spiritual darkness have caused Haiti to be the poorest nation of the Western Hemisphere. It became an independent nation in January 1804, when the slaves fought for their freedom and renounced their bond to France. This is the only country that has gained its independence through a bloody revolution by slaves.

There have been fifty-five presidents since 1804, only ten of which served the full term of four years. There have been many assassinations and coups d'état.

It is only second to the US in longevity of independence. In those two hundred years, it has never been free from tyranny, repression, political conflict, racial animosity or economic hardship.

- **Size:** Haiti is the size of the state of Maryland. Haiti has 10,714 square miles with a population of nine million. Maryland has 12, 407 square miles with a population of five million.
- **Language:** French and Haitian Creole
- **Religion:** Roman Catholicism (85%), considered the state religion; voodoo (85%, intermingled with Catholicism), proclaimed a legal religion by Ex-President Aristide in 2003; and evangelical Christianity (10-15%). In the past voodoo was a hidden religion, but now it is more prevalent and open in its practices.

The people: Haitians are simple people, an estimated 49% live in absolute poverty, meaning living on less than a dollar a day. In spite of their poverty, they love to laugh and share jokes and stories. They are family oriented. Haitian proverbs are used in every day conversation:

Kay koule twompe solèy, men li pa twompe lapil.

A leaky house can fool the sun, but it can't fool the rain.

UNDER THE RUBBLE

*"HE who dwells in the secret place of the Most High
Shall abide under the shadow of the Almighty."*
—Psalm 91:1

Tuesday, January 12, 2010, started as a normal day. We were busy throughout the day with ministry activities, not aware of an impending catastrophe.

Later in the afternoon, the phone rang. "Hi, Mom how is everything?" asked Rachel. We talked for a while.

"Well, it is that time of day," I said at last, "I need to work out. I'll call you later."

I went to the bedroom to put on my tennis shoes. The exercise machine was on the second-story porch of our house. It was almost five o'clock.

Suddenly, a loud, rumbling sound came out of the South. Patrick, in the second-story family room, stood up and immediately saw half of our house go down. Darkness! The floor underneath him was gone. The cement roof came down on top of him. His arm was pinned under iron bars, and a large cement slab lay on his back. He was sitting on one hip with his back curved forward.

Immediately the air was filled with blackened dust from the falling buildings. People were screaming and running from houses. The exercise machine fell from beneath me. As I was falling, the huge almond tree outside was swaying precariously towards the house. I tried to hang on to something. There was nothing to hold on to! Then a slab of cement hit me. I felt my foot being severed.

I was afraid to move. I saw blood gushing from my leg. I quickly removed my shirt, made a tourniquet, and tied it around my leg. When the ground stopped shaking for a moment, I tried to devise a plan, as is my normal reaction to any circumstance. But this one was beyond my ability to fix.

"Patrick, where are you?" I yelled.

"I'm here, but I can't come to you. My arm is pinched under the iron," he shouted. At least he was alive!

"I can't come to you either," I shouted back. I only saw one small opening above me toward the direction of Patrick's voice.

Buildings were falling everywhere. Soon the ground started to sway again. I heard more crying and the sound of people running from buildings. I thought Jesus is coming and the end of the world is on us. Then I realized it was an earthquake, and I thought of our children. They would hear about it on the news and be frantic, wondering where we were and if we were safe.

In thirty-eight seconds, what we had known as normal was gone.

There were three others in the house with us: Cherline and her two brothers, Rosano and Clerveau. Cherline had been living with us for the past ten years. Rosano was a student at a local high school. Clerveau, a worker for the mission, had returned with Patrick from the village where they had been working. Cherline and Clerveau were in the back side of the house. There were some walls damaged inside Cherline's room, but they were able to escape without harm. Clerveau pulled Rosano from under the debris immediately. He was not seriously hurt.

As I sat in the pile of broken cement, I heard Clerveau calling from below, "Barb, crawl to me. I can help you get out." I couldn't see him. He kept calling, "This way. Look this way." Finally, I turned my body towards his voice, and I saw a larger opening.

I dragged myself toward the hole. To get out faster, I removed my tennis shoe. I was sure my foot would stay inside my shoe. To my surprise, when I removed my shoe, my foot was just barely connected to my leg. With my foot painfully dragging, I inched toward the opening. When I finally reached it, Clerveau pulled me through, and carried me across the street, laying me on the sidewalk. Once again the ground began to sway.

Utter confusion surrounded me! I lay there in shock. My mind was racing. What had happened to Patrick? Would we be able get him out? How could I move? Soon someone offered to take me to the hospital. Cherline went with me.

The ensuing darkness put a halt to the feverish attempts of Clerveau and Rosano to free Patrick. He spent the night alone under the rubble. Alone...except for God. Clerveau and Rosano spent the night nearby in the yard. From time to time Clerveau handed a small bag of drinking water down to Patrick through a small hole. Later he would tell me, "All through the night I felt the ground shaking. I cried out in pain and begged God to take me Home. "I sang 'God is so Good' again and again in English and Creole, and heard people singing and praying all through the night."

When I arrived at the hospital, there was no room in the inn. So they laid me on the ground in the parking lot, where I stayed for the rest of the night and the next morning. A crowd of more than a thousand people were either lying on the ground or milling around. With only one doctor on staff, no one received help. I continued to hemorrhage. If I moved, I left a pool of blood. There was no water or pain medication available.

All during the night, people were crying out in pain. Some were calling out names trying to find family members. Once in a while, I heard a shout of joy when people were reunited. There were also painful cries…then silence. Too silent, and we knew death had taken another person.

I felt utterly alone! In my agony I battled to stay calm. My thoughts were rambling, How will I ever connect with Patrick? How will he know where I am? How will he find me? In my agony, God gave me a peaceful rest during the night. Maybe sleep, or maybe unconscious, but I awoke the next morning surprised that I had rested so well in spite of my cement bed and no pillow, neither a blanket to cover myself.

Across the ocean, the news traveled quickly. Morgan, also a missionary kid, called Rachel, who was living in Oklahoma. "Are you watching the news?"

"No. Why? What's going on?" Rachel asked.

"There was an earthquake in Haiti. It's serious," she replied.

Rachel phoned her brother in Florida "Agape! Agape! Have you heard?"

"Heard what?" he answered.

"There's been an earthquake in Haiti!"

Frantically, they tried to contact us all night long with no success.

This, I will never forget. As I was lying there, suddenly people were screaming "Amwe! Amwe!"(help, help). They were running away from the hospital. I hadn't felt the ground move. Why are they running? I turned my head toward the hospital. In the sky was a huge, white, tube-like cloud moving horizontally toward the hospital.

When it was above the building, three finger-like appendages came out of that tube and moved over the hospital. The fingers swayed to and fro, but never moved on staying the duration of the night. As daylight came, the cloud slowly disappeared. People have asked what I thought this was, I have no idea. God has not given me an answer.

As daylight came, Clerveau and some friends began working to free Patrick. Other friends and neighbors came to help in any way possible. They started chipping away the cement, but soon they realized that their efforts would not be enough. Patrick called out to them, "You are working too far from me. You need to make a hole closer."

Later he called again, "Hey guys. Go to the mechanic's shop where the car is and get the jacks. We can to try to lift the roof enough to release my arm."

A couple of them rushed to the shop. Everything was locked, and the mechanic was not there. They jumped the gate, broke the window of the vehicle, and got the jacks. But they were being watched by a policeman who held them at gun point, thinking they were thieves.

"This is our vehicle. We need the jacks to help our friend who is under his house," they explained. The policeman didn't believe them, but he let them go and followed them until they reached our house.

With the jacks, they started lifting the fallen roof very slowly. This process was very dangerous, as at any moment more of the roof might fall on Patrick. Little

After 18 long hours Patrick was pulled from out of the rubble

by little they continued their work, until the release was close at hand. Friends stood by watching, crying and praying. Abelard, Patrick's only cousin, and remaining immediate family member, stood by weeping.

While people were helping Patrick, I was trying to go to Blue Ridge Mission where my cousin was working. "Cherline, please go to the street to find a taxi to take me to the mission."

After some time she returned. She had not found a taxi. After lying there for some time, I asked her to try again. This time when she returned a man came with her. He looked at me and said, "Let's carry her to the street. Maybe someone will show mercy and take her where she can get help."

He picked me up, and carried me to the sidewalk, and he laid me on a dirty piece of cardboard. The sun was hot. People had used the wall behind me to relieve themselves. The smell was sickening. All this time my foot was open, dangling, and still bleeding.

As I lay on the sidewalk I was comforted by a familiar face. "What are you doing here?" Marley asked.

"I spent the night here but need to go to Blue Ridge Mission. We are trying to find someone who can take me," I replied.

"I am so sorry. I am without my vehicle today. Do you have money to pay a driver?" he asked.

"No," I replied, "but the mission will give them money when I arrive."

"Take this money," he said, placing it in my hand.

Then another acquaintance passed by, "I will go to the mission and get a vehicle. Stay right here. I will return." I stayed there for a while, but he never returned.

Finally, a man agreed to take me to the mission. His wife had broken her leg in the quake, and he needed to take her to a clinic for treatment. We went to the clinic where people were receiving treatment in a trash-strewn yard. The building was cracked, but still standing. One doctor looked at my leg, and said he could treat it. But all he could do was clean and bandage it. This helped, but I was still bleeding.

When we finally arrived at the mission, I was over-joyed to see my cousin, Berniece. She cried out in joy when she saw me. "Oh Barb, it is really you! I'm so glad you are here. I was so worried about you."

"I am very glad to be here. I need help. I can't walk" I said weakly.

"Don't worry. We will carry you," she assured me.

I left a trail of blood as they carried me to the house. The recliner offered to me was a welcome sight - so much better than cement and a piece of cardboard.

After eighteen long hours, a dust-covered Patrick was lifted out of the darkness into the light! It was ten-thirty in the morning, the day after the quake. His arm was numb and very swollen. A friend borrowed a vehicle to take him to a clinic. On the way to the clinic, they passed by the hospital to search for me, but I had already left.

Back in the States, our children were having their own nightmare. There was little phone communication in Haiti. They finally received news that Patrick had been freed from the rubble, and that I was in a hospital somewhere. They were desperate to find a way to Haiti.

God was already at work on their behalf. A close friend called them and said, "Please, go to Haiti to find your parents. I will buy the tickets. Please go." That was all they needed to hear.

Along the streets, on his way to a clinic, Patrick saw unbelievable sights. The country he once knew had changed overnight. There were bodies everywhere—some lying along the streets, some hanging from buildings. When Patrick saw the volume of deaths, his first thought was, "Today hell has been enlarged." A heavy burden consumed him: he knew he must work harder to share the Gospel.

After passing several clinics destroyed by the quake, Patrick was taken to the home of John, a missionary friend. But John wasn't home. A lady nearby saw Patrick and offered him a grass mat on which to rest. She bathed him and gave him water and soup. She was "an angel unaware" who God had prepared to care for his needs. Later John returned home, and found Patrick.

Our children were receiving conflicting reports about our conditions: "Although your dad was trapped under the house, He has no injuries. Your mom is going to a hospital in Santo Domingo. She has a broken foot. Nothing serious."

"Mom," Cherline said, "I heard that they got Patrick out, but I don't think so. We haven't seen him or heard from him. I think they just told us this so we wouldn't be afraid."

"Do you think he died? I don't think so," I replied, "I think he is out. We will find him." I said the words confidently, but my heart wasn't so sure. By early-afternoon, we still had no news of him. Some men from the mission went to our house to find him, but he was no longer there.

Finally around four o'clock, Berneice came to me, "Barb, we have a gift for you." In walked Patrick! I was ecstatic! But I could see that he was terribly sick. This reunion wouldn't last long. As the day passed into evening, Patrick's condition worsened.

On Thursday morning--two days after the quake—Patrick was in critical condition. He kept saying he needed an I.V. He felt life ebbing from him. Meanwhile, my foot was turning black; infection had set in.

Another missionary friend, Keith, came to Blue Ridge when he heard of our situation. "I have called a mission plane, and they are reserving two seats for you to leave this afternoon."

"Oh thank you," I answered, "What wonderful news."

"Be at the airport at four o'clock this afternoon," he said as he left.

Clerveau and Rosano who were with us at the mission, returned to our house to search for things. Patrick had told them in which 'rooms' they might find some valuable documents. A few hours later, they returned with our passports, Patrick's resident card, our bank cards and our credit cards. The exact documents we needed to leave the country!

In the meantime, Agape and his friend, Michale, were making preparations to fly from Tallahassee to the Dominican Republic. Because there were no commercial flights into Haiti, Rachel and her husband, Pat, were flying from Texas to meet them in the Dominican Republic, via Puerto Rico. When they landed in Puerto Rico, Pat received a call from the military that he needed to return home immediately. He turned around, and Rachel continued the trip to Santo Domingo. Agape, Michale, and another friend Curt arrived in Santiago at midnight. Rachel didn't make it until five o'clock Friday morning. The men picked her up. They planned to buy a few supplies and drive to Haiti.

We tried to call Rachel and Agape. We were cut off before we could tell them that we were leaving Haiti. We could hear them saying, "We are coming. We will be in Haiti soon." My heart sank. They were coming and we would be gone.

When we arrived at the airport, Loren, my cousin's husband, went in to find the plane, but one of their workers informed him, "We don't know anything about taking them on our flight. We don't have any seats left." What a disappointment!

Another friend, Michael, who was working at the airport, saw Loren and gave him more news, "Take them to the cargo building. Agape Flights is coming to take them to the States." We breathed a sigh of relief. We had a way to leave for the States. We were encouraged, but only for a moment.

Loren took us to the cargo building. Michael came to our car and said, "Stay here until I come to get you. We are trying to connect with the plane." We waited. Soon he returned with another message: "There are over thirty planes circling, and we lost contact with your plane. Stay here until we find it."

Again, Michael returned with news. "Military doctors are here, and will check you." A soldier came to the car, took one look, and told the men to carry us into the building. As soon as we were inside the building, eight doctors buzzed around, threw their medical bags on the floor, and started working.

They tried to start an I.V. on Patrick, but his veins had collapsed. A life line was inserted into his chest. I heard one of the doctors say, "His arm will need to be amputated." My heart froze. Though his arm looked bad but I didn't think it was severe enough to merit amputation. But I could see that Patrick's condition was not good.

Doctors also helped me, but there was little they could do except bandage my foot. One of them said, "This foot looks bad."

A Canadian Military plane had been loaded, and was ready for take-off. One of the soldiers asked the pilot if he would consider taking us to the States. "We cannot do that. We have not been ordered to land in the states."

A US soldier begged the pilot to reconsider. "This is a life-and-death situation. If you do not take them, they will die."

Finally we were loaded onto the plane on our way to the United States. We landed at Homestead Air Force Base and were air-lifted to Jackson Memorial Trauma Center in Miami.

On Friday morning, as Rachel was buying supplies to bring to Haiti, she received the most distressing call, "Your parents are both in critical condition. They have been taken to Miami. You need to go there immediately. They both had amputations." After three sleepless nights her emotions were frazzled.

Rachel, Agape and Michale headed back to the airport, praying for a flight back to the States. They were given the last available seats on the four o'clock flight, and arrived in Miami two hours later. They carried a heavy burden.

In Sarasota, Florida, Dale and Mary, my sister and brother-in-law, worked all night trying to find us. One phone call led to another. With each call, their frustration heightened. First they were told that we had been taken from Haiti to a hospital in West Palm Beach. Contacting every hospital there, they got the same answer everywhere, "We have no one by that name." The search continued.

Finally on Friday morning they were assured that we were at Jackson Memorial. When they called they were told, "We have no one by that name." As Dale kept pressing, the person asked him, "Why are you searching for them? Are you family?" So they knew we were there, and started the drive to Miami.

In the ER, the nurse had told me, "You and your husband will both need surgery. When you wake up tomorrow morning, you will be in the same room."

The next morning I woke up in a private hospital room, alone. No one was there. In the maze of my memory, I remembered what the ER nurse had told me. When my nurse came in to check on me, I asked, "Where is my husband? He was supposed to be here with me."

She looked at me and said, "I don't know about a husband. I didn't even know you had a husband. He is probably in surgery."

Puzzled, I said, "No, we were both in surgery during the night, but he wouldn't still be there. He was supposed to be in my room this morning."

"Well, I don't know," she said, and walked out of the room.

With the anesthetic still in my system I dozed off and, woke up again several hours later. The nurse came in, and again I asked, "Where is my husband?" Her answer was the same. I looked at her with determination, "Go find my husband. I want to know if he is dead or alive." She left the room.

Several minutes later, she returned, and said, "He had complications and was admitted to Intensive Care."

Little did I realize how near death he was. This separation lasted two long weeks. Patrick had his right arm amputated. I had lost my right leg below the knee.

When Dale, Mary and my mother arrived at the

hospital, they went to Intensive Care to see Patrick. They were not allowed into his room until they answered many questions. "How are you related? Are you the closest relatives?"

Dale replied, "No, they have two children, but they are not here yet. I'm his brother-in-law." Of course, it was a strange answer. After all, Dale and Mary were white and Patrick, being Haitian, was black.

Then they asked Dale a most disturbing question, "Would you be able to give permission for life support treatment?"

"Well, I would rather not, but as a last resort, I would," he answered. They were admitted to his room, not expecting to see him in such critical condition.

When the children arrived at the Miami airport Friday evening, God had already arranged for someone to be there to pick them up. A stranger, Zenaida brought them to the hospital. In fact, Zenaida and her husband provided a home away from the hospital for Rachel and Agape during our entire stay at the hospital.

When our children first saw their dad, they were shocked. They later told me, "We left his room, sat on the floor in the corridor and wept. We prayed harder than we had in a long time."

Patrick's Crush Injury (Rhabdomyolysis) caused all the toxins and proteins to pass into his kidneys, causing kidney failure. According to the doctors, he was going to die, unless there was an intervention. Dialysis treatment was started with triple the amount of fluid that would normally be given. This treatment flushed the kidneys, but then fluid filled his lungs resulting in respiratory arrest. His life hung in the balance. Day by day we waited and prayed.

God prepared many people to help in our time of need. One of those people was our dear friend Kaye. She came to the hospital within a few days, and remained the entire time we were in the hospital. She helped in any way she could for as long as we needed her. She was the backbone the children needed. She helped them organize, advised them when needed and put stability into their lives. She kept our spirits up, our prayers up, and humor in the day.

Slowly, oh so slowly, Patrick began to show improvement. His kidneys starting working again, but he was still on the respirator. Every day when Rachel and Agape visited him, they sang songs in Creole, prayed for him, and told funny stories. He didn't respond to them. They felt sure he heard them but was unable to respond. One day Agape said, "Mom, I think God and Dad are talking a lot."

Hospital staff and other visitors in the Intensive Care Unit had their eyes on Rachel and Agape. One day a visitor asked the nurse, "Who are these young people? Kids don't do this for their parents." Without knowing, our children were leaving a testimony.

Although I had the initial amputation on Thursday night, I had three more surgeries on my leg. Every other day, I was in surgery. My foot had been very infected, and there was concern that infection could be spreading. Finally, after the third surgery, the incision was closed.

I loved my nurses. Every day they would come to hear my story. God's faithfulness was very evident. Our joy and humor had some people perplexed.

One person asked me, "Don't you ever cry and get angry over your situation?"

"Of course," I said, "I weep over the country I have known for twenty-nine years. It will never be the same again. Am I angry? Yes! Now I have to buy a pair of shoes, and can only use one."

Some were curious at the joy I had. That offered more opportunities to share Jesus.

Humor was an integral part of healing. When a nurse checked my back and saw all the bruises and scrapes, she said, "Oh my, it looks as if a wall fell on you." We used that phrase many times.

My hair was a mess, still dirty and dusty with "rubble-grubble." One of the staff was congenial, and sent a hairdresser to help me. He kept asking me, "Am I doing it right?" Finally, I said, "You're the expert; you should know if it is right." I wasn't prepared for the next remark, "I am not accustomed to clients that talk. Most of mine are dead."

After eight days, I was given permission to see Patrick. As I was wheeled into his room, I saw a man I barely recognized. He was so swollen from the fluids that his whole body was disfigured. Yet, the children were encouraging, "Mom, he looks so much better than he did."

I had to leave the room. I couldn't control the tears and the fear I felt. I was afraid that the Patrick I knew would never be normal again. I didn't want to return to his room because it was just too difficult to see him in this condition.

A few days later, the children encouraged me to go see him. "He will know you are close, Mom. It will help him heal." Praying for courage, I decided to take their advice. A surprise awaited me. I approached his bed, and whispered his name, "Patrick, I am here." He moved his eyes. Then the moment of moments, he turned his head and lifted his lips for a kiss. Oh, what a moment that was! I don't know who was happier, the children or me. We were ecstatic to see his improvement.

The ventilator was removed on the fourteenth day. It was a crucial moment: if he could not breathe on his own, a tracheotomy would be performed. We watched the clock. Every moment and every hour were precious. After eight hours, we celebrated! He was breathing on his own.

While he was recovering in ICU, I was adjusting to having only one leg—learning how to walk with a walker, balancing on one leg to wash my hands, and getting dressed after a bath.

We had a decision to make. When should we tell Patrick that I had an amputation, too? He was waking up more often.

"My arm is gone. Why did they amputate it?" We knew the moment had come to tell him about mine.

I went to his bedside, "Honey, your arm is gone. So is my leg." He turned on his side, lifted his head, and then looked at my leg. "It's okay. We will work together."

I responded, "Yes we will. When you need an arm, I will give you mine. When I need a leg, you will share yours."

My trips to see Patrick were funny at times, especially with Kaye pushing the wheel chair. The normal way to Intensive Care was to go outside, and then to the next building. Kaye found another way that she was sure would be a shorter walk. I was sure we were lost, but she kept saying, "Just trust me." We ended up in the morgue!

When Patrick came out of sedation, one of the first things he asked for was Chinese food and Burger King. This was a moment of victory—he had remembered some favorite foods.

The fight wasn't over. It was a difficult battle for him to detox from the morphine. He ate non-stop and slept a total of five hours in six days.

I kept asking myself, "Will the man I married ever be the same again?" After many days, he began to be more like the Patrick we knew.

Life will never be the same. As Patrick said one day, "I am thankful for my amputation. We can reach people with God's love in a different way. We now understand others who have gone through the same experience."

Now quality of life has a new meaning. Our children were afraid they would lose both parents at the same time. Patrick and I didn't know if we would have each other again. Life is precious, and not guaranteed for to-morrow. We have only today.

Except for the grace of God, we would not be here today. But God went before us, behind us and beside us. He gets all the praise and glory.

Our thanks reach out to all who made our recovery so much easier. You blessed us with notes of encouragement, visits, meals, financial gifts, and most of all prayer!

Our house after the quake

AFTER SHOCKS

"God is our refuge and strength;
a very present help in trouble." —Psalm 46:1

This verse reminds me that God was my refuge and strength during the quake and afterwards. Although the preceding chapter, "Under the Rubble" is the story of the quake, I would like to share some of the miracles we experienced during that time. These certainly were daily reminders that we were in God's hand.

When our son, Agape, went to Haiti for three days while we were in the hospital, he went to see what had been our house. It had been a large two-story building made of blocks with a cement roof. The quake brought the house down to ground level. Agape walked the area that had been the kitchen. As he described it, "It was as if someone had put everything in a huge blender, mixed it up, and poured it on the ground."

When Agape returned to the states, he told us that he had been able to crawl underneath some of the house. He said, "I found find pieces of tile and then I knew what room I was in. I saw the hole where Dad had been lifted out."

Then he looked at me and said, "I saw the hole where you crawled out."

"How do you know that was the place?" I asked.

"Mom, I saw your blood trail." He said.

When we arrived in Homestead Air Force Base, the immigration officer came on the plane. I gave him our passports. Then he asked for Patrick's green card. "It is in his billfold in his back pocket." Patrick was sedated at this point, and not able to get it. "I believe you; don't try to get it," he said, as he returned the passports to me–the kindness of strangers was one of many blessings.

Clerveau and Rosano had also returned with our laptops and a few articles of clothing, which had been packed in a duffle bag for traveling. In the hospital, Rachel opened my laptop, turned it on, and it worked! Patrick's laptop had had his cell phone on the computer between the top and the keyboard. It had not shut securely. Even with that, it worked when we turned it on!

The men realized that the back of the couch had held the roof from completely falling on Patrick. Out on the porch where I had been, there was an old window air conditioner which we had never used. It had held the roof and kept me from being crushed.

Five years ago when I broke my hip and had surgery, the doctor warned me, "Be very careful on the Haitian terrain. If you fall, it will break your hip again or displace it." I think that although this was the hardest fall I could have experienced, my hip never hurt me. Ironically, it was my right hip, which was on the same leg that was amputated.

During that first week in the hospital, I thought of another miracle. My glasses had stayed in place, even after all the rumbling, shaking and falling. How strange is that!

Six months prior to the quake, I had been told by a doctor that I was legally blind in my left eye. He discovered a macular hole in my retina and told me I needed surgery. But the story doesn't end there. While in Tallahassee, I went to another eye surgeon. He gave me the same diagnosis. After several appointments the doctor said, "This doesn't happen. Your eye is healing itself." Being a Christian, he said, "It's the power of prayer." Several weeks later, there was even better news. The macular hole was gone! Another one of God's miracles.

God graciously provided a home for us when we left Miami. Our friend, Joan, shared her home for four months. She cooked meals, ran errands, and loved us back to health.

Last but not least is the miracle of life. Several months before the quake, I had been doing some research for a good vacation spot to celebrate our 25th anniversary (April 26, 2010). We hadn't taken a real vacation for many years. Our travels always integrated speaking engagements, family visits, and mission activities. I was thinking of the Grand Canyon or the Rockies. The quake took all those hopes away. How could we celebrate now? Going to the doctor and recuperating didn't seem like fun – certainly not a vacation! Then God touched my heart, "You have the greatest gifts of all: Life and each other."

Thank you, Lord. Help us to live each day as if it were our last.

Call to Missions

*"...Fear not, for I am with you; Be not dismayed,
for I am your God. I will strengthen you,
Yes, I will help you, I will uphold you with
My righteous right hand." —Isaiah 41:9-10*

As a young girl missionary stories were very exciting to me. But I was raised not being taught the importance of mission work. The first book on missions I remember reading was "Through Gates of Splendor" by Elizabeth Elliott. I re-read it several times. I could hardly put the book down!

As a teenager, I had a deep desire to go to the Indian reservations in Canada. That desire rested in my heart for several years, and God opened doors to send me on my way. I served on the reservation as a short-term missionary for three months. During this stay with the Cree Indians, the seed of missionary life was planted in my heart. Although, I was sure that God would bring me back to the Cree one day, He had other plans.

Ten years later, after dodging and detours, I was called to missions. As I was reading in Isaiah 58:6-9, the words practically jumped off the page!

Is this not the fast that I have chosen: To loose the bonds of wickedness, To undo the heavy burdens, To let the oppressed go free, And that you break every yoke? Is it not to share your bread with the hungry, And that you bring to your house the poor who are cast out; When you see the naked, that you cover him, And not hide yourself from your own flesh? Then your light shall break forth like the morning, Your healing shall spring forth speedily, And your righteousness shall go before you; The glory of the LORD shall be your rear guard.

I felt the Spirit of God speaking these words to my heart. A specific country, people group or region weren't clear at that point. I continued to pray.

Waiting on God can be trying. After all, I was ready to go anywhere. God knew my heart, and He knew I was not yet prepared for what lay ahead.

One day, two years later, the phone rang.

"Barb, would you be willing to go to Haiti?" asked a mission board member.

Stunned, I answered, "I would need some time to pray about it."

"Can you please give us an answer within a week?" he responded.

"What? One week? I can try..."

At the end of that week, I had my answer. I was scared

to say "yes," but I was more frightened to say "no." Six weeks later, I was on my way to Haiti. At that time, I thought I'd be back to the US after a year. Twenty-nine years later, I finally see that the Creole phrase, "Si Dye Vle" ("if God wants") is truer than most of us realize.

I WILL NEVER LEAVE YOU

"Be strong and of good courage, do not fear nor be afraid of them; for the Lord your God, He is the One who goes with you. He will not leave you nor forsake you." Deuteronomy 31:6

The first time I stepped onto Haitian soil, I felt at home. As I walked out of the airport into a drenching rain, Eris, the missionary I would be working with, picked me up like a sack of sugar, and carried me across the street to his vehicle. Water was up to his ankles, and he wanted to protect me from getting soaked.

It was already dark when we arrived at the mission house. Miriam, Eris' wife met me at the door and welcomed me into their home. Miriam would be my friend and teacher as I learned the language and culture.

They had a large two-story house, with iron works on the windows and doors. (I learned later that was not just decor, but protection from thieves). I felt like I was in a maze. Nothing felt like home. My bedroom was on the second floor. Once settled, I switched off the light and crawled into my single bed. Soon I heard the eerie beat of drums in the distance. I didn't find this especially comforting!

After my first night, I realized that sleeping late was not a part of Haitian culture. Long before I was ready to leave my bed, I heard the merchants calling out their wares (bread, sugar, eggs, brooms, etc), the shoeshine boys ringing their bells, and the knife sharpeners blowing their whistles.

I descended the stairs to an open doorway and entered the large kitchen. On the far wall was a small propane tank beside a stove. I thought this was quite dangerous to have the propane tank inside the house, but no one else seemed to notice. There was no hot water for washing dishes, and limited ice for drinking water. All drinking water was purchased in five-gallon jugs, carried home on the shoulder of the yard boy who was responsible for keeping the yard cleaned, running errands, and mopping floors.

Kitchen duty sounded easy until I realized I couldn't even ask for things. There was a Haitian girl to help me, but I couldn't converse with her. One thing I will never forget: the smell of garlic frying in oil over a charcoal fire. Not a pleasing smell at all!

Grocery shopping was not a simple task in Haiti. Small poorly-lit grocery stores, (if there was lighting at all) made it difficult to find items. Items were not properly classified on the shelves. There wasn't a choice of brand names or prices either. I needed to learn the money system. Haitian currency is based on the gourde which is five gourdes to a Haitian dollar.

Fresh fruits and vegetables were purchased at street markets. My skin color was definitely a disadvantage when negotiating prices. There were merchants with large baskets of fruits and vegetables on their heads, running down the streets, yelling their prices, hoping I would purchase from them. Those sitting along the streets immediately jumped up, pushing and shoving to get to me first.

So began my first years in a foreign land—my boot camp. If God would have given me all the details before I went, I wouldn't have stepped out of the boat. He had only asked me to take the first step.

You know you have lived in Haiti when...

You clean bugs from the rice.

THE VOICE

"...whoever calls on the name of the LORD shall be saved." Romans 10:13

"How old were you when your grandma started taking care of you?" I asked Patrick.

Patrick replied, "I was too young to remember. I was only told the story."

Patrick was born in Jeremie, a town on the western peninsula of Haiti. His mother moved to Port-au-Prince with her four sons. Soon the little ones started dying. When his grandmother realized his brothers were all passing away, she came to take Patrick, who was the oldest of the boys. Patrick was eight when his mother died. He never knew his father.

His grandmother, a staunch Catholic, went to mass every morning on her way to the open market where she sold coffee and other goods. She loved Patrick as her own son. She was very poor, but did all she could to provide the best education for him, sending him to a Catholic school.

One of Patrick's favorite antics was to take coffee from the thermos after his grandma left the house, but to avoid a confrontation with Grandma, he added water to the thermos, so the coffee wouldn't be missed!

He was required to attend mass every Sunday. Not only did Grandma require it, but so did his school. When Patrick was twelve, he was required to go to his first confession. Being very shy, he didn't know what to say. So not knowing what sin he committed, he created one to confess. He hated the church at this point because he felt the church was the cause for lying at confession.

He continued to attend school for several years, but there were problems in the school that finally caused him to leave. Since he was no longer a student, he also refused to attend mass. He observed many fallacies in the church and turned his back on God and became an atheist.

When he turned 14, his grandma sent him to Port-au-Prince to live with his aunt. There, he became involved with boys who were bad influences. He learned karate to prove his strength, and then used his training to fight in Mardi Gras. Girls became a wonderful addition to his wild life.

Although Patrick loved to read and study, books were a rare commodity. There wasn't money to buy them, even if one could be found. At every possible opportunity, he would borrow books from friends. One day a Christian lady moved in with his aunt, and Patrick saw a Bible on the table.

He knew what the Bible was but had never owned one

or even looked at one. As a Catholic, he was never encouraged to read it. A principle he had learned in school was to start reading a book at the beginning. He didn't know the Bible consisted of many books. He started reading Genesis, and soon became enthralled with the stories.

Still an atheist, he saw the book was different from others that he had read. As he read about Abraham, Isaac, and Jacob, he realized that this book didn't protect its heroes. These were great men of God, yet they committed great sins. The Bible showed it all. He shared the stories with friends.

He continued reading through Exodus, Leviticus, and Deuteronomy. With each book he began to understand life in a different way. He also became more convicted of his own sinful life. When he read the book of Job, he learned how patient Job was in the midst of his suffering. In Psalms he learned how to pray. In Proverbs he learned some practical principles for living.

God was waiting for him in Ecclesiastes. By now, he was feeling quite miserable, knowing that there was a God and that he needed to repent of his sins. He still wasn't ready to surrender his life. In Ecclesiastes 11:9 he read, "Rejoice, O young man, in your youth..." He was very excited realizing that this verse was particularly for him...he was a young 19 year old. In this verse, the words "young" and "youth" appeared several times. He now wanted to see what the Bible had to say to him.

"..and let your heart cheer you in the days of your youth." Oh yes! The word youth again! This is for me! He read on, "Walk in the ways of your heart and in the sight of your eyes..." What? I can do whatever my eyes and heart want to do? God really understands me.

Being young, his eyes found a lot to see and his heart followed. He became his own philosopher. He concluded, Whatever I read before now was for the older people. I am young, and God says I can do whatever I want.

He closed the Bible and was anxious to go meet some of the pastors who had tried to tell him of his sins. He was ready to show them in their own Bible that he was not required to repent.

As he was sitting in his one-room, tin-roofed hut, thinking who he could talk to first, he heard a voice. Birds walking across a tin roof make noise, but he was alone in the house. No one was on the roof, yet, the voice came from above. It was clearer than if someone had stood in front of him and spoken. "Patrick, open the book, I am not finished yet."

He opened the book, and realized in his excitement, that he had not finished the verse. The rest of the verse was heart-rending, "but know that for all these, God will bring you into judgment." The Word of God pierced his heart. He almost regretted having been so happy about the first part of the verse. Now he needed to accept the last part, too!

At that point, he gave his life to the Lord. He has been preaching and teaching the Word of God ever since—for over thirty years.

HANDIWORKS OF GOD

"The heavens declare the glory of God; and the firmament shows His handiwork." Psalm 19:1

Village life. No horns blaring. No planes or helicopters flying overhead. There was only the music of roosters crowing, goats bleating and donkeys hee-hawing, and the sweet sound of children's laughter as they played singing games in the mission compound yard. The children had no toys but they were very content playing with ropes, pebbles, a ball or playing group games.

Although I loved the simplicity of village life, it was also very lonely for me in the first years. I was not fluent in the Creole language then. With the language barrier, conversation with the natives was limited. I was the first foreigner who had ever lived in their village. I spent many afternoons building relationships—playing games, sharing a cup of coffee, or sitting with the village folk.

Some days the loneliness was almost unbearable. My heart ached to talk with someone who understood me and my mission. God was the one who understood me the most.

The natives did everything possible to make me feel welcome. Each afternoon, Junior would bring me a cup of coffee from his mother's house. Every Sunday morning before the service, a lady brought me bread and coffee.

I remember one of those lonely days. I tried to read, pray, or take a walk, but I really needed a "bosom" friend. My tears flowed freely. I cried as I went up the steps to the second story open porch. I stood on the south side of the porch and looked out over the beautiful ocean.

On this lonely day, God gave me a wonderful gift. Over the water was the most beautiful rainbow—fully arched! It was a sunny day, with hardly a cloud in sight. It had not rained for many days. The rainbow was a promise to me....God's reminder that He would always be with me. I was not alone.

One of my favorite pastimes was watching the stars. I spent many hours on the roof at night gazing at the heavens. The stars seem to dance. I have seen shooting stars often as they travel across the heavens, and wondered if they were on a mission from God. Were they going someplace specific by command, or was God simply giving me a show that has remained imprinted on my mind forever?

The Celestial Star Choir sings every note to perfection. After all, they do have the perfect Maestro.

You know you have lived in Haiti when...

you're the only "bleached out" person in a
crowd of a thousand.

ONE STEP AT A TIME

"Your Word is a lamp to my feet, and a light to my path." Psalm 119:105

In the middle of the day in Haiti, the sun was bright and hot. Patrick and I had a list of things to accomplish, and one of them was to walk to Demeline, a village up the mountain from Mayette. It was a forty-five minute hike, but since we walked along a creek and trees shaded the area, it was usually a beautiful trip.

The trail crossed the creek about five times, which meant hopping across the creek on unsteady rocks. I'd hiked this trail many times before and had always enjoyed it… But I am getting ahead of myself.

Evening came, and we still hadn't left for Demeline. Of course, most Haitians, especially in the village, have developed a sixth sense: cat eyes. Americans, like me, haven't quite gotten the gift. Even without flashlights, the group with me seemed to walk quickly and steadily.

Gripping my flashlight, I following carefully behind. The first part of the walk was on a canal approximately eight inches across. One side was the mountain wall, but the other was a ravine, falling hundreds of feet below. It would only take one misstep to go tumbling off the canal edge and be a pancake on the ravine floor.

Next came the dance on slippery rocks through the stream. The last fifteen minutes was almost a straight crawl to the top of the mountain. There were loose stones, but at least it had no trees, and the bright moon guided us along our way. The stars were diamonds in the dark. They welcomed us to the summit. What a majestic view. It was God in all His incredible majesty. Not only did the stars welcome us, but the people of the village were waiting for us, too.

This dark hike was a perfect example of God being the light to my path. As I held my flashlight to see just a few steps in front of me, I didn't worry what was ahead. I'd concentrate on what I could see. God didn't have to show me what was ahead. He showed me one step at a time. I never would have arrived in Demeline that night if I had not continued to take ONE step at a time. Was I frightened? Yes, but as long as I kept my eyes where the light was shining, I knew I would be safe.

That night, we had a wonderful visit with the Demeline people. We walked home on a different path; but with my flashlight and my Jesus both shining so strongly, my path stayed well lit until we made it home.

Swingin' Rats

"Truly the light is sweet, and it is pleasant for the eyes to behold the sun;" —Ecclesiastes 11:7

Life on the mission field affords experiences that one never finds on the home front. It helps to learn to laugh at yourself, accept embarrassment and even allow others to laugh at you.

One of those times was on one of my first trips to the village. This particular one was located 120 miles from Port au Prince. The dirt, mountain roads tend to shake every muscle in your body. I was exhausted, when I arrived not to mention, extremely dirty from traveling the distance in a truck with the windows open. It seemed like every grain of dust from on the road was on my face.

My sleeping quarters at the village was a small room at the back of the church, which I shared with three native girls. There was only one small cot for sleeping. The unpainted walls were lined with large cooking pots, sacks of rice and beans, boxes with various supplies for the feeding program, and dishes piled on top of all of the boxes. On one wall was a makeshift closet. The space between the cot and the supplies was quite limited, only room to step one foot in front of the other. The room was very dark. There was no electricity. At night, we "felt" our way around the room.

As the guest, I was invited to sleep on the cot. The other three girls squeezed a quilt on the floor and bedded down for the night. Soon they were asleep, breathing heavily.

I had not yet been initiated into the wonderful world of rats, but I was about to be, in a totally dark room. Just because there was no walking space for humans, this did not stop the rats one iota!!

Soon they were on the trail, scampering over the dishes and knocking them down. It sounded like a war zone.

Then came recreation time: The rats were swinging on the hangers. Oh my! This American gal just couldn't lie down and sleep. Nor could I leave the room, because the girls had locked the door, and I couldn't see!

I finally decided sitting on the bed was no different from lying down. Obviously the rats were accustomed to an audience. It didn't faze them. So I laid my head down and was almost asleep, when a rat ran across my forehead. EEEEK!

My greatest embarrassment came the next morning as I stepped out of the door. A group of fifteen village folk were sitting in the yard, laughing. "The blan (white woman) couldn't sleep because of the rats." I guess the girls weren't as sound asleep as I had thought!

You know you have lived in Haiti when...

Rats are more common than dogs!

THE ROOSTER, GOD'S PROVISION

"Therefore do not worry, saying, 'What shall we eat?'
or 'What shall we drink?' or 'What shall we wear?"
Matthew 6:31

Clouds of dust filled the air as we traveled along the endless dirt road to get to Puits Sales. Thorn bushes, rocks and potholes were the primary objects of scenery along the way. At last huts appeared as we entered the village.

The desert-like village of Puits Sales was to be "home" for several years. The village had no fruit trees, gardens or stores to buy food. The spring for drinking water was three miles away. Donkeys carried jugs of water, or women balanced a five-gallon bucket of water on their heads.

Eris, the pastor I was working with, would bring me some groceries and basic needs from the city every two weeks. How grateful I was to his wonderful wife, Miriam. She knew exactly what to put in those care packages.

One week the pastor didn't come. Several days passed, and still no one came. I was down to my last few dollars. Then I saw Patrick (who was also working with us in the mission) meandering across the yard. I was excited and sure he had come to bring me my supplies. I couldn't have been more wrong!! He brought nothing, only news that Pastor Eris was sick and couldn't come. My heart sank.

I had been very hungry for an egg. An egg would be a nice diversion from my diet of bread and honey. I didn't tell Patrick about my craving.

The next day as Patrick was leaving the village to return to the city, he met a man who wanted to sell him a rooster. Not knowing my dire situation, he said to the man, "Go tell Barb to pay for the rooster, and keep him for me."

My mind went berserk! What? Give my last few dollars for a rooster I don't need! Absurd!

But I had no chance to discuss this disgusting situation with Patrick. He had already left the village.

Later that day, a lady came to visit me. She was carrying a chicken under her arm. When she found me, she handed me the chicken, "Barb, I want to bless you today. Here is my gift to you."

The heart's immediate response was, I can't take a chicken from her. She has hungry children to feed. But I also didn't want to deprive her of the blessing of giving. After a few minutes, she left.

Immediately God nudged my heart, reminding me of my hunger for an egg. I sensed the whisper in my heart,

"Barb, now you will always have eggs. I have provided you with a rooster and a chicken." I never thought that God would answer my prayer for an egg this way.

You know you have lived in Haiti when...

You hear roosters crowing at one o'clock in the morning.

MEETING PATRICK

"...And a threefold cord is not quickly broken." —
Ecclesiastes 4:12

I was never one to be excited at the thought of marriage. Mission was on my heart, not to mention traveling and helping people. I was sure single life was for me. Finding a husband was not even on my prayer list!

I had been in Haiti for a year. In Haiti, I usually went to the same church every Sunday evening. This particular evening a young man who I had never seen before, sang a solo. When the pastor starting preaching and I forgot about the soloist.

The next week Pastor Eris asked if I would like to go to the village of Puits Sales with him and a group of young men who were going to preach a week-long revival service. Since I was sitting in the front, I wasn't looking who was in the back of the vehicle. When we stopped along the road, a young man came to my window and introduced himself. "Hello, my name is Patrick." I recognized him as the one who had sung the solo in church.

We still laugh about our week together in the village. I hardly knew Creole, and they didn't know much English. We spoke in signs and wonders to each other. We signed, and then wondered what it meant.

Soon after that, Eris asked Patrick to help him in the ministry. Now I saw him every day. He was friendly, but I suspected he wanted my friendship so he could learn English. I saw this as an easy escape from learning Creole.

I was skeptical of this young man. I thought he was like all the other Haitian "friends" who only wanted a free ticket to the states. Besides, he told me he was engaged. I prayed that God would take him out of my life. Instead, working together caused our friendship to grow deeper. As I got to know him, I realized he was quite different. He was very sincere in his walk with the Lord. Having no earthly father figure, Patrick had begun to know God as his father.

One day an American came to Haiti for a medical clinic. He asked Patrick to be his translator. Patrick told him that he wanted to finish his training as a printing machine operator. The following year Jim returned to Haiti.

He had returned to take Patrick to the states to learn the printing trade. When they went to the consulate to apply for a visa, Patrick was denied. Jim was sure he heard God telling him to bring Patrick to the states. He called the consulate to try again to persuade them and was told to return with Patrick and they would issue him a visa.

Patrick lived with Jim and his family in Florida for almost two years. I had been in Indiana on vacation, and was returning to Haiti by way of my sister's. While there I realized that Patrick was only five miles away, and we knew that God had more in store for us than a simple friendship to learn English.

Several months later, I returned to the states so we could meet my parents who lived in Indiana. I wasn't sure how they would react to a cross-cultural relationship, much less give their permission for marriage. When we arrived at the airport, my parents were there to meet us. My mother was surprised when Patrick greeted her, "Hi, Mom."

We received my parents' blessing. Patrick, wanting to make sure he was accepted, wrote my mother a letter. She was so thrilled that she shared it with her neighbors and friends. He had told her that they must be wonderful parents because I was such a wonderful daughter. We still wonder if Patrick was being a bit conniving, but it worked!

A GRAIN OF WHEAT

"...unless a grain of wheat falls into the ground and dies, it remains alone; but if it dies, it produces much grain." John 12:24

"Barb, Barb, come quickly, Eclusia is hemorrhaging!" I left the school office quickly, and followed Joe to a nearby mud hut. As I entered the hut I heard moaning. My eyes searched the darkness. A woman was lying on old rags that covered the grass mat. The only other articles in the hut were a few beaten-up pans and a rickety wooden chair.

"What happened, Eclusia?" I asked.

"Yesterday I was walking home from the spring with a bucket of water on my head. When I saw Joe coming down the road, I knew he would be mad at me for carrying such a heavy load so I quickly lifted the bucket from my head. When I did so, I felt something pop inside my stomach."

"And you have been bleeding since?" I asked.

"I am pregnant, but I think I already lost the baby."
She replied.

Since it was too late in the afternoon to find a public
vehicle to go to the hospital, they planned to see a doctor the next morning. The next morning I took some
money to pay her way to the hospital, but she was too
weak to move.

I sat down on the dirt floor beside her. Eclusia
reached for my hand, and held it. "Would you adopt me
and be my friend?" She pleaded. She was very lonely.

From time to time, I offered her water, milk, or tea,
but she vomited everything. She was burning with fe-
ver. Her body was trembling. I felt she had an infection
and probably needed blood.

Village folks passed by to visit her. "Eclusia, you
know God is knocking at your heart's door. He is giving
you another chance. Don't you see He loves you? Barb
wouldn't be here if He didn't love you," Brother Frank
said.

"Yes, now I know He loves me," she replied. She
closed her eyes and rested.

A sick smell permeated the hut. Flies were buzzing
everywhere. She never complained. She only wanted
me there with her.

Three days passed, and each day, she became weaker.
If I left to go home to eat or take a shower, she called
for me. She was afraid to go to sleep. She had slept very
little since becoming sick.

I knelt on the floor beside her. "Eclusia, you know

God loves you. Why don't you want to give your life to Him? Jesus died for you. He will forgive your sins."

"I will make that decision now," She said, weakly. Some neighbors came and prayed for her. Eclusia prayed. "I belong to Jesus, He has forgiven my sins. I have peace," she told us, and then went to sleep.

I had gone home for the night. Sunday morning I returned to the hut. Another lady and I carried her outside, sat her on a chair and gave her a bath. She seemed a little better. She was more alert and not trembling as much.

After her bath, we laid her down again. I read the chapters of 1 John 3 and 4 to her. From time to time, she would say, "Praise God. Glory to God." Sunday afternoon was uneventful, but by evening she had become very thirsty. Her abdomen was hard and distended.

My legs were aching from sitting on the floor so much. I was hot, and could hardly endure the sick smell. My body felt contaminated. I left for the night, promising to return the next morning.

Monday morning I worked in the school office, but checked Eclusia from time to time. She was suffering chest pains. I sat on the rickety chair and sat her up against me so she could breathe more easily. It seemed that she was losing ground.

Mid-afternoon I returned to the mission compound to finish my office work. Minutes later, someone came running. "Please come. She passed out. We can't wake her up!"

I entered the hut, I could see that she had passed

away. The ladies were still shaking her body, calling her name, "Eclusia, Eclusia please wake up!"

Softly I said, "Ladies, our friend has passed away. She cannot wake up."

They looked at me with questioning eyes. They realized I had spoken the truth. They left the hut, screaming. Another lady and I covered her body and left the hut, closing the door behind us.

Immediately people started wailing. Joe was uncontrollable. He ran around the hut and tried to go through the window. Suddenly he crawled up a tree and hung upside down. The people of Haiti hold many superstitions regarding death. Someone opened the door, blew a whistle inside, and then closed the door. This was to keep the spirits away.

The eerie sound of a wooden bugle announced the start of the "wake." The Haitian way to celebrate a "wake" is to laugh, dance, sing, and play dominoes all night. This is to take their sorrow away. From time to time the bugle was blown to make sure the spirits didn't return. At daybreak, the wake ended and all was deathly quiet.

The funeral and burial were scheduled within twenty-four hours after death. There is no preserving a body in the village. Eclusia was a very poor person by the world's standards. She had few friends. Her parents lived on another island. The hut belonged to her uncle. The man she lived with belonged to another. She even had to share the grave where she was buried.

In her death, Eclusia was like a grain of wheat. Although she had no earthly riches, she was greeted by all of heaven who rejoiced because a daughter of the king had come home. All of heaven rejoiced because a child had come home.

Note: I wrote this story many years ago, soon after it happened. It was found under the rubble after the quake.

THE DARK OF NIGHT

*"In God I have put my trust; I will not be afraid.
What can man do to me?" —Psalm 56:11*

Political uprisings are almost as common as breathing in Haiti. Demonstrations show a dislike or disapproval of government decisions. Although common, we are accustomed to them, but try to be careful in the areas where there are problems. Even though caution often defines the way we live, sometimes we unknowingly walk right into an uprising.

One morning we left the village of Mayette in Southern Haiti for our home in Port au Prince. It is 120 miles which takes six hours driving. At 3:00 P.M. we were at the half way mark of our journey. We noticed vehicles had stopped up ahead, but since traffic is common, we thought nothing of it.

Suddenly, a young man jumped onto the side step of the truck by Patrick's window, "Look, there is a situation up ahead. They are stalling vehicles. I will help you through." Not having the time to think about it, Patrick shrugged and kept moving.

When we came to a semi-truck parked to block the highway, the young man riding on our sidestep ordered, in a not-so-kind of a voice, "Pull your vehicle over there. Turn the engine off and hand me the keys."

"This vehicle has no ignition key, sir," Patrick informed him.

"You are lying. Give me the key," the man demanded.

"Sir, my vehicle does not use a key," Patrick tried to assure him.

The terrorists checked the vehicle and realized there was no key.

"Everyone stay in your vehicles! No one leave!!" commanded the terrorists.

They kept their eyes on us. The threats kept coming, "Let's slice all their tires." Much later we heard one say, "We will set this vehicle on fire."

More and more vehicles were being parked. Time was ticking away, and we had some urgent needs. There was no food, water, or toilets. We were finally allowed to find a bush or tree to relieve ourselves.

Night was settling in. Our son was home alone expecting our return. Finally, faking a nap on the seat, we called home without being caught using our cell phone. We did not want our phones to be taken away.

The night was dark, but not as dark as the atmosphere around us. I was terrified, especially when I heard that they were going to set our vehicle on fire. I decided to escape on foot, not sure where I would go as home was far away.

When Patrick heard of my plan, I was strongly reprimanded. "Barb, where is your God? Where is your faith? You will cause us all to be shot." I felt ashamed.

Finally at 3:00 A.M., twelve hours later, we were told to leave. I asked Patrick, "Are we sure it is safe to leave?"

He replied, "We do not know this, but if we are commanded to leave and don't, we know we will be shot."

We were free. We arrived home safely at daybreak.

Praise the Lord for His promise in our
darkest of nights.

THE SCAVENGER HUNT

"Then He took the five loaves and the two fish, and looking up to heaven, He blessed and broke them..."
Luke 9:16

Construction projects have been a major part of the mission work in Mayette. When we first started our work there, we slept, ate, and held services, and mobile clinics in small thatched-roof structures. However, as time went on and the ministry grew, it was essential that we have other buildings. Frequently a work team would come help the natives—lightening the workload and quickening the pace.

One particular week, a team arrived from Florida. The old army truck, more specifically known as "Jehu" (we weren't sure if it was named for the speed of the truck or the speed of the driver) was loaded with all the food, water and construction supplies needed for framing the second story of a building.

Each member of the team found a spot for the long six-hour drive to the village. Some stood to get a good view of the scenery. Others were sitting on top of boxes, plastic containers, or squashed in the corner of the seat. The wooden seat wasn't a soft landing when bouncing along the dirt road. Our muscles were hurting from all the jostling and bouncing, thanks to the many potholes and rocks.

Places we never saw along the road is McDonald's, Burger King or a gas station with a restroom. The only McDonald's was eating our sandwiches from home, sitting under a shade tree. A bush or tree is the Haitian version of a roadside rest area.

After arriving in the village and unloading the truck, everyone was exhausted. Each person was finding a spot for his or her sleeping bag or air mattress. Most chose to sleep on the roof where it was much cooler with a myriad of stars for their cover.

The next morning after a good cup of Haitian coffee, the work began. We carried lumber, nails, and tools up the ladder to the second story of the building. There was the sound of joyful laughter and singing as workers pounded nails and cut lumber. Haitians joined in the activities. There is no language barrier in laughter.

The team had been working for several hours when the leader yelled down below, "Bring us more nails."

"Hey, where are the nails?" one of the men asked.

"I saw them on the back of the truck," someone answered.

"I can't find them. I don't see them anywhere. They are not on the truck." Several men started the search for nails. No nails could be found.

The situation was brought to Patrick's attention, "There is no store or town nearby to buy more nails."

"What can we do now?" asked the team leader.

Patrick advised them, "Go ahead and use all the nails. When they are gone we will work on something else."

The work started again. Workers started checking the ground, and a few nails were found. Others reached into their construction aprons and pulled out a few more.

Every few minutes we heard, "Hey I found another nail in my pocket." Then another called out, "I found a nail in my pocket!" There was excitement in the air. A scavenger hunt was underway for nails.

At the half-way mark, there were NO nails. But the nails continued to be in a pocket until the work was completed!

The Lord had performed the miracle of the nails. It seems God not only multiplies bread and fish, but He's also good with nails. Natives and foreigners joined hands for an electrifying praise service.

You know you have lived in Haiti when...

The water you wash your clothes in is
dirtier than the clothes.

EXCEEDINGLY ABUNDANT

*"Now to Him who is able to do exceedingly abundant-
ly above all that we ask or think..." Ephesians 3:20*

I was exhausted. I was traveling to Florida for a Women's
retreat. My flight was from Port au Prince to Tampa,
then to Tallahassee. I planned to sleep in the Tampa airport instead of spending the money for a hotel.

We left Port au Prince on schedule, but when we arrived in Miami we were held on the tarmac for an hour
and half until the gate was cleared.

I rested on the plane. I was so tired I could have spent
the night there. I read my book without interruption—
unusual in my mission life.

This delay caused me to miss my connecting flights. So I
got off and went to the service desk to reschedule my flight.

"Sorry ma'am, there are no more flights to Tampa
tonight. The next flight is tomorrow at six o'clock. We
will provide vouchers for a hotel and meals," the desk
attendant said.

She handed me vouchers for the Hyatt.

My mind was racing; The Hyatt! I had never stayed at a Hyatt. Are you kidding me? What luxury!

I was in for another surprise when I got to the hotel. "Are you a single traveler?" the desk clerk asked.

"Yes, ma'am," I replied, barely able to hide my excitement.

She was checking for rooms, then said, "We have one room left which is a suite for a single person. The room is on the seventh floor. Is that ok?"

"Yes, It's fine," I replied, squelching my joyous laughter.

A suite? Is this ok? Need you ask? I was like a little child with a big gift at Christmas.

The room had a beautiful view, overlooking the city. The suite was larger than a Haitian hut. It was a complete house—living room & dining room, kitchenette/bar, bedroom, and a huge bathroom. I almost fell asleep while taking a shower. Can you imagine? Hot water! The meal voucher provided the grandest buffet I have ever seen. The only missing link was Patrick.

In my room, I prayed, "Lord, I know you can do exceeding abundantly above what I can imagine, but isn't this a little over the limit? And for free? Provided by YOU."

I arrived at the retreat the next day, rested and refreshed.

Matt 11:28 "Come unto me, all you who labor and are heavy laden, and I will give you rest."

Red and Yellow, Black and White

"I will praise You, for I am fearfully and wonderfully made; Marvelous are Your works, And that my soul knows very well." Psalm 139:14

Raising a family in a cross-cultural marriage has its challenges. Children adapt to the culture they live in, and then try to "fit in" to the culture when visiting another country.

The diversity of culture, habits, and ideas that flavored our home provided us with a wealth of experiences. For clarification, I believe some habits are universal—dirty clothes on the floor stay there for the wife/mom to pick them up. Loose notes scattered around the house are not to be discarded by the wife. Wife talks to husband engrossed in his computer work, who is not hearing a word. Isn't life interesting?

Our children learned both Creole and English languages simultaneously. Rice and beans were a daily fare. Pizza, ice cream and potato chips were a rare treat. In

Haiti our tropical fruits—bananas, pineapples and mangoes—were definitely much better.

On one of our visits to the states, we were staying at grandma's house. Our children tasted the milk and were sure it was spoiled. They only knew the taste of powdered milk. Bananas were served for breakfast. Rachel, being quite young at the time, whispered in my ear, "Mama, what are we eating?"

I replied, "It is a banana."

"No, mama, it looks like a banana, but it isn't a banana at all."

I assured her, "It is a banana, but just doesn't taste like the ones at home in Haiti." She was not convinced it was a banana.

Our children, like most children, were full of questions about life, people and family. They loved their daddy's stories and jokes. Agape kept our family laughing.

Then one day Agape asked a "profound" and unexpected question, "Why did God make daddy black, mama white, Rachel brown and me yellow?" Our multicolored family had never been mentioned. We didn't know he even noticed. He was only four years old.

Then came the next question, "Why is daddy black, and not like us?"

"We love daddy the way he is. This is how God made him," I explained.

"But, why? Why is he not like us?" the questions continued. We tried different ways to help him understand.

Finally, thinking I had an excellent response, I said "Agape, Daddy is really like us. We are all alike on the inside."

Shouldn't this have satisfied the little mind? Wrong! Agape was quiet and pensive. Then suddenly and very brilliantly he said, "Daddy why don't you turn your skin inside out?"

There was no answer for this. Only laughter.

You know you have lived in Haiti when...

When you thought you earned a suntan, but you were only dust-covered.

DEVIL'S MOUNTAIN

"I will lift up mine eyes unto the hills, from whence cometh my help. My help cometh from The Lord, which made heaven and earth." Psalm 121:1-2

Only a Haitian knows the moves of another Haitian driver. Traffic laws and speed limits are respected when it is convenient. They can easily make a two-lane street into four lanes without any engineering experience or degrees. You have to squeeze in and make yourself known with a horn. A horn is almost more important than brakes.

Trucks and buses take curves on the wrong side of the road. Potholes decorate paved roads, as well as donkeys, cows, bicycles and pedestrians. Speeding trucks and buses are the cause of many accidents.

Once while traveling on one of these roads, the brakes gave out on our big army truck going down the mountain. The driver was having a difficult time keeping the truck in the middle of the road as it went faster down the mountain. There was no oncoming traffic for which we were very thankful. Finally at the bottom of the mountain the truck began to slow down. It was a close call.

On another trip, we were driving to the village on a mountain road that was very rocky. A vehicle with a four-wheel drive was imperative to travel this road. We had just crossed a rocky river bed and were ready to make the two-hour trek over "Devil's Mountain." The name of the mountain should have been a warning. The incline from the base of the mountain was very steep and rocky.

As we started our ascent, Patrick realized he had forgotten to put the four-wheel drive into gear. As he was changing gears, the brakes gave way. We started speeding down the mountain.

The land rover was rocking from one side to the other, "bouncing" over rocks, continuing the downward spiral. There was no way to control it. Fortunately, at this point there was no ravine on either side of the road.

Suddenly it leapt over a large rock and leaned dangerously on two wheels. At that moment, we fully expected the vehicle to turn over completely. To our surprise, it found its way on all four wheels again and continued going.

Finally it hit a rock wall behind us and came to a sudden stop. We were stunned. When we realized the vehicle had really stopped, we were sighing with relief! A few of us had minor bumps.

There was an iron rod across the back bumper that had protected the vehicle from any major dents and damage.

"Will the vehicle start again?" someone asked.

Patrick walked around to evaluate the situation. "I

don't know, but we are far from help in these mountains."

After we had all taken our seats again, Patrick tried the engine; it purred like a kitten—as if nothing unusual had happened. When we started up the incline again, we realized that our run down the mountain hadn't been nearly as far as we thought. But it had been far enough!

You know you have lived in Haiti when...

You drink one cup of coffee in the morning and it keeps you ZAPPED for the day!

A WALK TO REMEMBER

"And I have led you forty years in the wilderness.
Your clothes have not worn out on you, and your
sandals have not worn out on your feet. You have
not eaten bread, nor have you drunk wine or similar
drink, that you may know that I am the
Lord your God." Deuteronomy 29:5-6

B eing single during my first years in Haiti I was ready
for every adventure I could find. I loved hiking the
mountain trails—the scenery, meeting people on my
hikes and the quietness of nature.

The village of LaBaliene sits in a valley with mountains surrounding it. I was visiting some friends there,
and we had planned the adventurous hike to Puits Sales,
the village where I was working. Besides being a very
long hike (8-10 hours), we didn't know the way over the
mountains to the village.

We were to meet our guide at four o'clock the next
morning. Our plans were set. To my surprise, at bedtime, the three other girls were getting cold feet over

our planned trek. They decided to cancel, and begged me not to go.

I was not going to give this up. "Whether you girls join me or not, I am going."

"The trip is too long to go on foot. We don't want to go." They said.

"We have already hired the guide. We should go." I was determined to go, and they were determined to stay.

The next morning at four o'clock, I met the guide, and so began my journey.

We walked over the mountains and through the woods. Little huts were scattered along the way. It was a beautiful walk.

Every so often, the guide asked, "Are you going to continue?"

I looked at him, not understanding, "What? Not go on?"

Again, he tried to convince me, "It is a long way. When we leave the mountains, the sun will be hot."

But I walked on. Many hours later, when we left the mountain path, and were on the more traveled dirt road, he was right, the sun was very hot! There was no protection. Not only was the sun very hot, but the road was hot and dusty. My feet were hot inside my tennis shoes. I estimated the walk would take another three hours. My water supply was running low and my food supply was definitely depleted.

The sun grew hotter and the road dustier. On we walked. Finally the guide stopped, looked at me and asked, "Are you ready to give up?"

I looked at him as if it was the strangest question I ever heard. "Kisa?" (what?), I asked.

"Well," he started mumbling, complaining about the situation.

So I told him, "I know the way from here, if you don't want to continue, you may return to your home."

Encouraged, He looked at me, and asked, "And my money?" "I'm sorry, sir, the deal was for you to be my guide to the village. If you cannot fulfill your end of the bargain, neither can I. Feel free to go, but there is no pay."

He sighed and walked on. He was quite unhappy.

When we were about thirty minutes from the village, I heard a truck coming. I knew this public transportation could get him close to his village from the highway. I decided to be merciful.

"Sir," I said, "I hear a truck coming. If you want to take a ride back to your village, I will pay you, and go the rest of the way alone,"

His eyes lit up. He was quick to take the money, but when he saw the amount, he said, "But can't you give me more?"

"No, this is the amount we agreed upon. You did a good job. Thank you very much," I said.

We parted ways, and I continued on.

My feet were burning from the hot dusty road. After eight hours of walking, I nearly passed out when I sat down. Then I had a surprise when I took of my shoes, and looked at my feet. They had big blisters and my tennis shoes had huge holes.

Then I remembered the walk of the children of Israel took in the wilderness for forty years.

Isn't God amazing!

A SACRIFICIAL GIFT

*"By this we know love, because He laid down
His life for us. And we also ought to lay down our
lives for the brethren."* 1 John 3:16

The tònèl, a palm leaf lean-to, was filled with young mothers holding their sick babies and a multitude of toddlers. In between cries and jabbering, mothers were intently listening to Manoune, a tall, slender Haitian lady, who was teaching the nutrition class. Malnutrition and diarrhea are the major cause of death in Haitian children.

After the teaching, we weighed the children and charted their progress. They were given a vitamin and a meal of rice and bean sauce or corn and beans with a glass of milk.

I enjoyed watching Manoune work with the mothers and children. She taught them so much. She loved her work, and put her whole heart into it. Every day I saw the same little girl with Manoune. She never went home, and didn't appear sickly, yet stayed with Manoune. Whose daughter was she? Where did she belong? Manoune wasn't married.

One day she told me the story:

"Marie's oldest brother was quite sick. Everyone knew he was going to die. Marie's family lived in a mountain village many hours away where there was no doctor or clinic. They heard about the feeding program here, so they brought him to this village for help. I gave him food and medication. Frequently they returned with the boy. He never healed completely. So I asked them to leave him with me so I could take care of him every day.

In time he got well and was ready to go home. His parents came to take him home. They felt indebted to me, but they had no money. I assured them that I didn't expect payment. I was only happy to help.

The parents decided to give their only daughter as a gift. They had four boys and one girl. I accepted their gift and promised I would give her the best of care. I raised little Marie as my own child. Her parents come to see her frequently."

They did not give her away because they didn't want her, but because it was the best gift they had.

Does this sound familiar? I think it is exactly what God did for us—giving us His only Son not because He didn't love Him but because we were so special to Him that He wanted us to have the best.

Marie? She grew up to be a beautiful Christian young lady. She is married to a wonderful Christian man and has a beautiful family.

You know you have lived in Haiti...

When you eat spaghetti for breakfast.

ENCOUNTER WITH A WITCH DOCTOR

"And do not fear those who kill the body but cannot kill the soul. But rather fear Him who is able to destroy both soul and body in hell." Matthew 10:28

Soon after Patrick became a Christian, he started traveling throughout the country of Haiti—preaching and teaching in churches. He also taught a weekly Bible study. Some from the Bible study group would frequently go to different areas to share the Gospel.

One day Patrick and some of his friends went on a "journee" (24 hour mission trip). They went to an area not far from the city. They walked the paths, singing and preaching as they went. Sometimes they were asked to enter homes to share the Gospel

Patrick was singing as he approached a house. The others were a little ahead of him preaching. Before he got to the house, an angry witch doctor came out yelling, "Stop the singing. You are disturbing the peace."

Patrick smiled and replied, "Sir, may I share God's love with you?"

"You are disturbing us. You need to leave," He yelled, even louder.

The rest of the group returned to see what the problem was.

"Sir I mean no harm, I am here to share God's love with you. I am on public ground. I am not on your property," Patrick said.

"No, I don't need to listen to you," He shouted, "I don't need you or God. Leave now."

Persistent, Patrick asked again, "May I come in and share God's story with you?"

"No, if you come in I will have you arrested." He threatened again. The man's anger was more intense.

Patrick stood his ground, "I'm not leaving. God loves you."

The witch doctor became angrier, but Patrick didn't run.

The man turned and commanded men standing near his house, "Go get my gun!"

Frightened, the others with Patrick said, "Patrick, we need to go. We are in trouble."

The witch doctor stood facing Patrick, waiting for his gun.

Then Patrick looked at the witch doctor and said, "You may get your gun, but I have a weapon more powerful than yours." Patrick was amazed at the words he heard coming from his own mouth.

When the witch doctor heard him speak of his own weapon, he calmed down. He assumed Patrick might be a member of the secret police.

"I didn't mean to hurt you," He told Patrick.

Patrick rebuked him, "Yes, you did want to hurt me." Then kindly said, "I only want to share God's love with you."

When the man saw that Patrick had no fear and spoke with love, he became very quiet. He listened as Patrick shared the love of God with him.

Then he told Patrick, "Many church people have come to preach to me, but they only condemned my actions. Today is the first time that I have heard how much God loves me."

The witch doctor didn't know the powerful weapon Patrick spoke of was a little Gideon New Testament tucked away in his pocket.

The man didn't give his life to the Lord that day, but the seed was planted.

STRANDED!

"Trust in the Lord with all your heart, and lean not on your own understanding;" Proverbs 3:5

Ignorance is not bliss, especially when it involves hurricanes. In 2008, there were four hurricanes in Haiti in three weeks. There is neither preparation nor evacuation for hurricanes. If there were an evacuation option, I wonder where Haitians would go.

Patrick left for the village and had planned to return home in three days. The rains and the winds started soon after he arrived in Mayette.

At home in the city, I realized these rains were more severe than usual. I checked the internet. A hurricane was on its way, and there was no way to warn the Patrick and the people in the village.

When the storm passed, Patrick called, "Barb, I must tell you I can't come home."

"What do you mean, you can't come home?" I answered.

He said "Every road is washed out, and I can't even leave Mayette."

My brain immediately kicked into gear, trying to find a way to get Patrick home. All my ideas hit brick walls. Patrick was stranded.

Fruit trees had been uprooted, animals died, houses and gardens destroyed. The area resembled an earthquake rather than a hurricane. Roads were now craters. Rocks had been washed in from who knows where.

They gathered fruit from the fallen trees. The animals that had died were butchered and cooked. After that food was gone they would have no more.

In a few days, the sun was shining again. Local men used their man power to make a road for Patrick, who felt strongly that God had him in the village to be an encouragement to the people. He was stranded there for a week.

Finally the road was passable. Mud painted his truck as he made his way through the potholes. At one place it took four hours to be dug out of the mud. As he crossed the river, the gushing water came up above the hood of the vehicle.

The driver of a large truck was watching Patrick cross this river. People had warned him not to go. When the chauffeur saw Patrick had no problems, he decided to cross too. Immediately his truck sank into a deep hole. That truck was stuck in the river for three weeks. Was it God who parted the waters for Patrick? We believe so.

Two hours after he came home the second hurricane hit.

You know you have lived in Haiti when...

A hurricane hits the village, and you didn't
know there was one on the way!

CROSSING THE LAKE

"When you pass through the waters, I will be with you; And through the rivers, they shall not overflow you..." —Isaiah 43:2

Hurricane Hannah ripped through the island, causing more damage than the three other hurricanes that had passed the week before. People were desperate, very hungry, and would call us every day from the village asking, "Do you remember we are still here? We need help."

Patrick assured them, "We have not forgotten you. We are praying for a road to open so we can get to you."

We had sent a truck loaded with food to them, but it couldn't get through. Finally, Patrick found passable road to the village.

Before the hurricanes, two friends from the States were scheduled to travel to the mission. We encouraged them to cancel, but they decided to come anyway. They really wanted to visit the village. After much effort and many phone calls, Patrick found a different route over the mountains to the village.

The truck was loaded and the men left for the village. Long after I should have had a phone call from Patrick, the phone was still silent. I began feeling uneasy. Finally in desperation, I called one of our pastors. "Has Patrick come by your house yet?"

He replied, "No, I haven't seen him."

"Oh no! He should have been in Mayette for a while already," I said.

Much later, he did arrive in the village safely, but only after a harrowing journey. The slippery mountain road was very steep and dangerous. The truck swerved from one side of the muddy road to the other. On one side were gardens, on the other side was a deep ravine, hundreds of feet below.

The truck swung into gardens, then back on the road. If they tried to stop the vehicle it would slide down the mountain. All they could do was keep the battle of the mud going.

After many hours, they arrived at the foot of the mountain. Someone saw them and asked, "What are you doing on this road? We never use this road when it rains, it is too dangerous."

Then they said, "Do you know that a few days ago two vehicles went over the embankment, and were never found?"

Then they realized how precarious this mountain trek was. A bit shaken, the men knew God's hand was definitely on them.

After several days in the village, they decided to find a

safer way home. The road that they would normally take had a big lake across it now. The waters continued to rise. With help, vehicles could go across. So Patrick opted to take this road home.

On their return home, they battled many mud holes once again. It took four hours to get out of one hole. It was dusk when they arrived at the lake.

A policeman stopped them, "You can't cross now. It is too dangerous to cross after dark."

Patrick replied urgently, "Sir, please, I have two Americans who need to get to the airport early tomorrow morning. We need to cross tonight."

"No way. Tomorrow morning at six o'clock we will take you across," replied the officer.

Patrick argued, "No. That is not early enough. We need to go no later than five o'clock. We have a plane to catch".

Finally the officer agreed. It was a long night. They were first in line to cross the next morning.

The engine was turned off, gear in neutral. While a few men pushed them across the lake, the water kept rising. As the vehicle was slowly moving across the lake, the water kept rising. Everyone was wet. In the middle of the lake, the water had risen above the dashboard. Luggage and boxes were water-logged. "Would the vehicle even run after taking on so much water?"

After they got out of the lake, they opened the hood, took out the air filter, and shook the water out. Then Patrick turned the key and the motor began to purr.

They arrived home at eight o'clock, with thirty minutes for a shower and the trip to the airport.

One of the men laughed and said, "If my pastor ever prays as he did before I left for Haiti, 'Lord, bless all of their adventures' I will cancel my trip."

You know you have lived in Haiti when...

Your vehicle is stuck in a mud hole, and it takes eight hours to pull it out.

BAG OF BONES

"Heal the sick, cleanse the lepers, raise the dead, cast out demons. Freely you have received, freely give."
Matthew 10:8

Walking along mountain paths, Patrick and some friends shared the Gospel at huts as they passed along the way. They had already talked to several people when a young girl came running from a mud hut, begging them to come and pray for a sick man.

As they entered the dark hut, a grass mat was barely visible in the corner of the room. Drawing closer, they saw a man lying on the mat. He looked like a bag of bones lying there—very thin and emaciated. He could not speak, and had been unable to leave his house in several months.

As Patrick looked at the man, he wondered in his heart, "Did the family ask us to come pray before he dies?" They prayed, and left the hut.

As they started down the path, a deafening scream came from the house. God urged Patrick to go back.

He told the others, "We must return to the house. He has a demon."

"How can you know that?" they asked.

Patrick explained, "Remember, the family said he was unable to utter a sound for months. Now he is screaming. We must return!"

Patrick and his friends had never cast out demons, but they felt God's power was with them. As they entered the house again, they started singing. The man was restless, as they prayed and read scriptures. After they sang praise songs, the man responded to them and told them his name.

They continued on their way for several hours before turning back for home. As they neared the hut of the sick man, they decided to visit him once more. When they arrived at the door, they saw the grass mat empty.

They thought, "Oh no, he must have passed away as soon as we left."

When they met a lady, they asked, "Where is he? What happened?"

She replied with great joy, "After you prayed, he immediately felt strength in his body. He left his bed where he had been lying for many months and went to his garden."

Praise the Lord!

CROSSING THE BORDER

"The LORD your God, who goes before you, He will fight for you..." —Deuteronomy 1:30

During the early '90's, Haiti was filled with political unrest, and as a result there was a siege on the country. The airlines announced their final flights out of Haiti. Many missionaries had left already.

I needed to make a decision. My parents were having their 50th anniversary celebration in August of that year. The last plane was leaving Haiti in June. We didn't know how long the siege would last.

Finally Patrick encouraged me, "Take the children and go now. I will meet you there in August."

"But how can you say that?" I questioned, "You don't know what the situation will be."

Again, he said, "Take the children now. I will find a way by August to meet you there."

Not too convinced of his promise, but knowing it was best for us to leave, I packed our bags. Our children were sad. Daddy was staying home, and we didn't know when we would see him again.

When we arrived at the airport, I handed the agent our tickets.

He informed me, "I'm sorry, but this airline has already cancelled all flights."

Patrick asked, "But sir, what can you do for us? Can you honor these tickets on another airline?"

He answered, "I don't know, and even if we could, I'm not sure there are seats available."

We waited for a long time. Flight time was minutes away. Agape was vomiting. Rachel was crying because Daddy was staying behind. Mom was wondering how she would manage. And yet we waited.

Finally they called our names to board the plane. It was the last flight, and we had the last three seats. We were very thankful those seats were right by the restroom.

We stayed in Sarasota from June to August, and still the planes were not flying in and out of Haiti. The anniversary celebration was to be the end of August.

One day I received the news that Patrick and Eris, whose wife was also in Florida, would cross the Dominican Republic border on foot and fly out of Santo Domingo.

"We are leaving the house now. I will call as soon as I arrive in the Dominican Republic," Patrick promised. Normally that should take only two hours.

I did not tell the children Daddy was coming. What if...? After six long hours, I still had not heard from him.

I was getting very uncomfortable. I called a prayer team. I knew something had gone awry. At bedtime, I could not contain my tears.

Rachel, eight years old at the time, asked, "Mama, why are you crying?"

"Oh, honey, Daddy is supposed to come, but I don't know where he is," I answered.

She looked at me, eyes filled with her child-like faith, and said, "Oh mama, don't worry, daddy will be here tomorrow."

Not wanting to discourage her with the gravity of the situation, I just didn't say anything.

Several hours after that, the phone rang. It was Patrick! The sweetest voice I had ever heard said, "Honey, we are coming tomorrow. We are fine. We have a story to tell."

What an experience they had! This was his story:

"When Eris and I arrived at the Dominican Republic border, we were told only US passports are allowed to cross the border. 'I'm sorry,' the officer said, 'But laws were changed a few days ago. Haitian citizens are not allowed to cross.'

"We left the Immigration Office at the border not knowing what we should do. Then someone came to our rescue with a suggestion, 'Look, I can get a motorcycle across the border to pick you up as soon as you cross. You will need to walk across.'

"The man continued, 'See those ladies at the border selling food? Walk there, and pretend to be buying food. When you see the cycle on the other side, quickly step across and get on the cycle.'

"We left our bags with the friend that brought us to the border, put on our sunglasses so as to have a different appearance and meandered toward the merchants. We pretended to buy food as we got closer to the border. As soon as we saw our escape cycle, we crossed.

"It was a small cycle. To avoid problems, the driver took us the through the woods, off the main route. We had not gone very far into the woods when a police-man stopped us, commanded in Spanish, 'Paseporte! Paseporte!' A bit shaken, but trying to remain calm on the outside, we handed him our passports. 'No, no, you go back! Go to jail.' He yelled. We stammered for a bit, but finally offered him money. 'No, no, go to jail! Not enough,' he replied.

"When we heard the words not enough, we felt hope-ful. We offered him more money, but he shook his head. We offered a bit more. He gave us a big smile and became very helpful. He even told us where to hide until we could get a vehicle to take us all the way to the Santo Domingo.

"We left the woods, and the cycle driver hid us in an empty house. He gave us orders, 'Stay here until another driver comes to take you the rest of the way to the city.'

"Sitting there, we wondered, Is there really another driver, or is this a trap?

"The longer we waited, the more we feared this may not have been a good idea at all. Was there another man, or was the next step prison? Finally a military officer came, 'Where are you going?'

"We replied, 'Santo Domingo, Sir.'

"As usual, 'I will need money.' Having no choice, if we wanted to get out of our current situation, we agreed to the price.

'Come with me,' he said.

"He led them to a compact car. We got in the back seat, our knees pushing into the front seat. No complaints, at least not verbally. The officer got in, propped the gun by his leg, and with music blaring, we were headed toward the city.

"We kept our eye on the gun. Every few miles we would stop at a check point. There was always the same command, 'Do not talk, do not leave the car.' With every passing check point, we sighed with relief.

"Finally, at a check point, the officer said, 'Get out, no more check points. Get on bus, and go to city.' Sweeter words, we hadn't heard in a long time! We felt free at last.

"Looking like street guys with our unkempt hair, sweaty clothes, and in dire need of a shower, we called a Canadian missionary friend in the city. After hearing our predicament, he invited us to his house. On our way, we both bought an outfit of clothes, since our clothes had been left behind in our luggage, but we forgot to buy a comb.

"The next morning we headed for the airport with our friend. Now we encountered our next obstacle. Because we did not have a legal entry stamp in our passports, we could not leave the country. Our friend took our passports to an official he knew and explained the situation.

After some convincing, he agreed to stamp our passports and to give us legal passage to the United States.

"Finally, we were called to board the plane, and sent on our way to meet our wonderful wives!

"We boarded the plane with a plastic grocery bag which held our few belongings. We should have bought a backpack, but decided the voyage was unique, so why ruin it with normal traveling gear? We used a dinner fork to comb our hair, since our combs were left in our bags back in Haiti."

"Looking back, I realized that God had used our eight year old daughter to reveal His plan for her daddy to find us.

You know you have lived in Haiti when

You're the only one on the beach with a swimsuit.

Surgery in Haiti

"...and the peace of God, which surpasses all under-standing, will guard your heart and mind through Christ Jesus." Philippians 4:7

The hospital room was drab green. In it was a single bed with an old plastic mattress, covered with a sheet. In Haiti, the family provides the bedding, food and sometimes water for the patient. It was the best room in the hospital: in addition to the bed, there was one chair and a bedside table, a bathroom, no towels, and most of the time no water. This was to be my room for six days. I feared the surgery scheduled for the next day.

It was November 2005, the day before Thanksgiving. It's as clear in my mind as if it happened yesterday. A dear friend with two other guests had been scheduled to arrive to spend the Thanksgiving weekend with us. We were very excited. I went to the store to purchase a few final items for dinner. As I was crossing the street to the store, I became the target for a bicycle coming down the wrong side of the street, full speed.

In a moment, I was on the ground in excruciating pain.

I didn't even remember Thanksgiving dinner. By the weekend, we knew I had more than a simple "bump". On Monday I made my first of many trips to the doctor.

After the doctor saw the x-ray, he said, "I am sure you have a fracture, but the x-ray doesn't show it. We will wait for the inflammation to pass, and then x-ray again."

After three weeks, I was told, "You have a fracture. The only solution is hip surgery." During those weeks I slept on a recliner. Lying flat in bed was too painful.

I sat in front of the doctor, put my head on his desk, and cried. "Oh Lord, what am I getting into?"

Having surgery in Haiti was not in my plans. I had heard too many horror stories—power going off in the middle of surgery, and no fuel to crank up the generator. Most incisions were double the size they should be.

My surgery date was set for December 23. Merry Christmas!

After I checked into the hospital, and settled in my room, a nurse came in to start an I.V. She tied a tourniquet around my arm, and inserted the needle. She forgot to release the tourniquet at that point, and blood spurted all over the sheet, my gown and my arm. Again I thought, "If this happens with a simple I.V., what will happen in the surgery room?"

Soon another nurse entered the room, "I see you have a cell phone. May I borrow it to call a doctor (not mine). We have no working phone on the floor."

"Oh sure," I replied. I felt I was at Disney World on Mr. Toad's Wild Ride.

Since a family member was required to stay with the patient, Patrick returned home to get pillows, sleeping bags, food, and water. Cherline, one of our Haitian "daughters", and Patrick camped out on the floor in my room.

The day of surgery arrived. We were all apprehensive. No one was talking. I tried not to show my fear to the others. The room was dark and dingy. Cement blocks were on the floor along one wall, but I wasn't sure why they were there. The only encouragement I had was seeing the wrapped sterilized surgery packs. At least, I knew their instruments would be clean.

As I was lifted from the gurney onto the surgery table, I was very aware of God's wings hovering over me and a peace flooded over me that I had never felt before. The Lord reminded me of this—Philippians 4:7, "and the peace of God, which surpasses all understanding, will guard your heart and mind through Christ Jesus."

I was given a spinal block, so I wasn't totally asleep. I heard doctors laughing and talking as they worked. Finally, I asked, "What are you doing? Building a house? It sounds like carpenters instead of doctors." That brought more laughter.

During the six days of my recuperation, I was never turned on my side. I wasn't allowed out of bed for five days. Even then, it was the surgeon who came and helped me, not the nurses. The surgeon had warned me, "It doesn't matter which hospital you choose, most nurses are lazy." In fact one night Patrick went out in the hall where he saw the only nurse on duty for that floor, sitting in a chair, her mouth wide open, sound asleep. By the time I was dismissed, my arms were so bruised from restarting IV's, they appeared to have been through a major battle.

A month after the surgery, I travelled to the States for more recuperation. Eight months later, I was back in surgery to repair what had been done in Haiti.

Only God knows if I would have faith to have surgery in Haiti again. Maybe like the first time, I won't have a choice.

A Legacy

"God is our refuge and strength, a very present help in trouble." Psalm 46:1

This verse has become a special comfort for me as I have lived on a foreign field, separated from my family.

The year 2005 afforded many unforeseen events. That year three aunts, one uncle, and two cousins passed away. This was also the year I broke my hip.

That same year, my sister called me at four o'clock in the afternoon. "Barb, Dad is in the hospital. The doctor says he won't live longer than twelve more hours."

"I cannot even get a flight out of Haiti in twelve hours." I said. "I will come as quickly as I can."

The next morning as I boarded the plane, Dad was still with us. At each connecting airport, I called for an update on his condition. I arrived at the hospital at midnight, thirty-two hours after receiving the initial call. God gave us five more days with our dad.

Those five days were very special. He was able to pronounce a blessing on each grandchild, except one, who was unable to be there. He had many visions during those days, and we were blessed as he shared them with us.

His heart was burdened that his nieces, nephews and their families were not saved. He sent my brother to share the Gospel with them one more time.

The last few days of his life, he was also no longer able to talk. He also could not raise one of his arms, but one day we saw him raise both arms as if he were leading a song. Perhaps he was hearing the heavenly choir.

After he died, one of the grandsons said to Grandma, with tears, "Grandpa is gone now. Who will pray for us every day?" Grandma assured him that she would take that part of Grandpa's ministry.

Dad left a legacy for us. He loved the Lord. He loved to talk about the Lord with others. I can still picture him standing by a field at the side of the road, talking to neighboring farmers. He was never too busy to lend a hand or speak an encouraging word.

Almost a year after his death, several people of the extended family were saved. A nephew, his wife, and their children gave their lives to the Lord.

The one phrase my dad used on a daily basis when he met someone—stranger or friend—was, "Well, how is your walk with the Lord today?"

May his legacy live on. We miss you, Dad.

GOD'S FLIGHT CONTROL

"For as the heavens are higher than the earth, So are My ways higher than your ways, And My thoughts than your thoughts." Isaiah 55:9

I was trying not to be anxious, but it was difficult to relax. I prayed, "Please Lord, keep my connecting flight waiting until I arrive."

I was flying from Florida to Indiana to meet my mom and sister, who were picking me up to go on to Illinois for a funeral. I was scheduled to arrive in Indianapolis, which was en route to Illinois. It seemed like a perfect plan.

The cost was quite important, so when I found a low fare, I quickly made the reservation. Still a bit perplexed at the low cost, I really checked the schedule. Now it made sense—Tampa, Charlotte, Washington DC, and then to Indianapolis. Since I enjoyed airports, I thought this shouldn't be a problem.

The flight from Tampa was on time. In Charlotte, we waited on the tarmac for take-off for thirty minutes. This would present a problem for my connection in

Washington, DC. In the air, I watched the time. I prayed that God would help me make my connection. When we landed in Washington, I had fifteen minutes to arrive at the gate, de-plane, and get to the connecting gate. It took ten minutes just to get to the gate. I had five short minutes.

As I left the plane, and ran to the gate. I heard an attendant call a loudly, "Are you Barb Lataillade?"

"Yes," I panted.

"Run through that door, and down the stairs. The plane is waiting for you!" she said.

As I ran for the door, a man was running behind me. "Ma'am, let me carry your bag." I handed him my bag, and we went flying down the steps.

When we got to the bottom of the steps, I found only a shuttle. "What? Where is the waiting plane?"

We got on the shuttle, and headed for the tarmac. There, waiting for us, was the plane ready to make the turn down the runway. While in the shuttle, the man looked at me and said, "Ma'am, you are the most important person in my life right now."

Shocked, I had replied, "Sir, I'm sorry, I don't even know you. How can I be important to you?"

He explained, "Because you had a boarding pass, they held the plane. I didn't have a previous reservation, but they allowed me on this flight because they were waiting on you.one."

The steps were down, the door opened, and we boarded. There were two empty seats. We took off. Clouds had never looked so good.

God had another surprise for me in Indianapolis. I went to baggage claim, knowing I would need to file a claim and return for my luggage. But my luggage was already there.

ELIYA'S STORY

Eliya never knew her father. He had died when she was very young. Her mother didn't have a job, only a small garden with corn and beans to feed her children. She wanted to send them to school, but she couldn't afford it. She had to make a decision.

"Erick, since you are the oldest child, and will soon be able to go find work to help us, I will keep you at home with me. Eliya, you are smaller. I will send you to live with your aunt," she said sadly, nearly in tears. "She can help you go to school. You can do chores around the house in exchange for her financial help."

Little Eliya was very sad she had to leave. She loved her mother dearly—loved to go to church with her.

Her aunt was Catholic, and there was no Christian influence in her home. After arriving at her aunt's house, Eliya learned that life was going to be very difficult. She had to work like a slave for her aunt! Although she was young, she was responsible for carrying water from the spring, sweeping the floors and yard, and washing the dishes. She also went to school.

Her aunt was very harsh and beat her often. If the work wasn't completed before she left for school, she'd get a beating when she returned home.

Sunday was no easier. She was forced to attend church with her aunt. She hated that church and refused to sing. She also got a beating for her attitude during church. This went on every Sunday. Finally, Eliya decided to pretend to like church to avoid the beatings. How she longed for her mother!

One day her mother came to visit. "Mama please, take me home with you," she cried "Pleeeeeaaaaase!"

"But, my child, I am not able to feed you or send you to school," she insisted.

"Please, Mama, I don't want to stay here. I'd rather be hungry than stay here," she begged.

But it was no use. Her mother thought it best for her to continue living with her aunt.

A few years passed, but the situation didn't change. One day her aunt demanded, "Eliya, wash these dishes. I am going out, and they better be done when I return!"

Eliya washed the dishes. She carefully washed each plate and cup until they sparkled. When her aunt returned home, she saw the dishes had been washed. Thinking Eliya wasn't watching, she took some of the dishes and soiled them again. Then she accused Eliya, "You did not wash these dishes. You disobeyed me."

"I did wash the dishes, and you know they were clean," Eliya answered.

"No. You have been disobedient," her aunt said angrily, "I will punish you severely for this!"

Eliya cried, knowing the beating that awaited her. But at that moment, she made a decision. I will not stay. I will go home to my mother.

In her aunt's absence, she ran home to her mother. Again, she begged, "Mama, I'm the only daughter you have. I can help with the work at home. Please let me stay with you. My aunt beats me every day."

After some convincing, they went back to her aunt's house, and told her, "I am taking Eliya home with me. She is twelve years old now."

Eliya was very happy to be home. She and her mother were very poor and made fun of by the neighbors. But this was better than being beaten at her aunt's house. Once again, Eliya went to church with her mother. It was wonderful!

Soon after she had returned home, she heard of a new church called Calvary Chapel in a nearby village. She searched for it and when she found it, where she heard wonderful singing and teaching. She heard about Jesus and gave her life to Him, and was baptized. She's been working in the church ever since.

Their neighbors still hate them, but for a different reason. Their hut had been damaged during a hurricane, and someone helped them rebuild it. The neighbors are jealous because they have a better house. God provides!

You know you have lived in Haiti when...

You come face to face with a
tarantula.

Worst Enemy, Best Friend

"But I say to you, love your enemies, bless those who curse you, do good to those who hate you, and pray for those who spitefully use you and persecute you..."
Matthew 5:44

He spent his days running around on the hot dusty ground and rocks. Little Robert lived near the ocean in a small one-roomed Haitian hut with his drunken father. When he was seven months old, his mother took him to his grandfather's house, but his grandfather threw him into the street.

Robert's father was unable to take care of him and tried to force Robert's mother to take back the baby. She refused. He finally found a woman to take care of Robert. She loved him as her own.

This boy grew up never knowing the love of his mother or his alcoholic father. As he grew older, he wandered away from home. One day while he was playing with his friends, he heard singing in a church, and started going to church every Sunday. When his father found out, he beat Robert severely. In spite of his father's threats, he continued to go to church. He was punished every week.

One Sunday, in the middle of the service, his father stormed into the church, grabbed Robert by the collar and dragged him home. His father yelled, "If I ever find you in church again, I will chop your head off!" Robert moved to another house, and continued to go to church. He hated his father, and saw him as his enemy. Alcohol had taken its toll on both of them.

When he was older, he was at a party when he heard singing across the street. A new church was having a revival. He went closer to the church. As he listened, he sensed a power holding him in place. At the end of the service, the pastor invited people to give their lives to the Lord. He went inside the church and gave his heart to Jesus.

When Robert was a young man, his father moved from the village to Port au Prince. He was active in gang fights. One day, the fight was so intense he was arrested and thrown in prison. While there, God started convicting his heart. He began to see how miserable his life was.

After he was released from prison, he started attending church. He finally gave his life to the Lord. He left his old friends and quit drinking. Now he attends church every Sunday.

After his father's release, Robert went to visit him. His father asked for forgiveness, and confirmed his love for him. They started to develop a new relationship.

Today Robert has a wife and a beautiful daughter. He is the pastor of the church that had conducted the revival where he was saved years before.

A Mother's Hatred

"I know how to be abased, and I know how to abound. Everywhere and in all things I have learned both to be full and to be hungry, both to abound and to suffer need." Philippians 4:12

"Amwe!" (Oh, help!). Eight year old Joseph was bouncing along on rough and rocky terrain. He was tangled in a rope and was being dragged behind a runaway cow.

A man saw the accident and caught the cow. Joseph was untangled from the rope. His condition was serious. His head was split open and the skin was laid back, exposing the inside of his head.

Medical help was far away, and vehicles difficult to find. Finally a vehicle was found, and he was rushed to a hospital a few hours away. At the hospital, the doctor took one look and said, "I'm sorry this is too critical for us treat here. You will need to go to another hospital." What he really meant was, I don't want to bother; he will die anyway.

They went to another hospital, and again were refused treatment. This doctor said, "His condition is too critical. He is going to die."

Not willing to give up, the driver and the man who had found him continued to a third hospital, several hours away. By this time Joseph was unconscious. The doctor examined him, "He is very critical, but I will do what I can, but I cannot give you any hope."

After several days, the doctor told them, "He will be brain damaged, and will be like a vegetable."

God had other plans. After fifteen days in a coma, Joseph started talking normally. Each day he made progress. He stayed in the hospital for six weeks. He still has a scar from this accident, but God healed him completely, and he is very intelligent.

Although Joseph was healed physically, he was very depressed. During all that time in the hospital, his mother never came to see him. She knew about his accident, but never asked about his condition. Joseph had deep wounds because his mother didn't love him.

At 17, Joseph searched for his mother. He wondered if she really did hate him. He had been told she gave him away at birth. When he found her, she acknowledged his presence, but without any welcome or conversation. She expressed no regret for what she had done.

Several years later, she attended his wedding. She did not congratulate her son or speak to him. She refused to eat the food offered to her. Culturally, to refuse food is a humiliation and shows rejection of the hostess.

Although his birth mother never showed any love for him, Joseph is forever grateful to the lady that loved him and raised him. It was she who sacrificed her life for him, not his birth mother.

THE WEDDING BAND

"Give to him who asks you, and from him who wants to borrow from you do not turn away." Matthew 5:42

The day was bright and sunny. It was a perfect day for a little boy to fly his kite—a homemade kite, that is. When springtime arrives in Haiti, many brightly-colored kites decorate the sky. Some fly high, while others get caught in trees, wires or bushes.

Today ten-year old David was ready to fly his. He climbed to the flat roof of the neighbor's house. This was an excellent place for a good wind to lift the kite.

Intent on flying his kite, David didn't notice how near the edge of the roof he was. He made one misstep and went crashing to the ground where he landed on rocks, receiving many deep cuts and bruises in his head. The doctor did not think he would survive his injuries. David was given no anesthesia before the doctor began stitching all the open wounds.

He was in the hospital for a week. He needed antibiotics and other medication, but his aunt had no money.

She had not remembered to take the money from her house. The hospital was too far away to return for it. Finally, in desperation, she found a pawn shop where she surrendered her wedding band as a security deposit, and received a loan of five dollars for the medication. Promising she would return to pay her loan in five days, she quickly went to buy the medications.

When David was released from the hospital, his aunt needed money for the bus fares. She finally convinced the bus driver to lend her the money for five days. As promised, within five days she repaid the money to the bus driver, and also the pawn shop where she retrieved her precious wedding band.

You know you have lived in Haiti when...

You've had nine flat tires in one trip to the village...and no local tire shop!

THE CURSE

"But love your enemies, do good, and lend, hoping for nothing in return; and your reward will be great, and you will be sons of the Most High. For He is kind to the unthankful and evil." Luke 6:35

Missoule loved school. She earned the best grades in her class. One day she became very sick. Her parents took her to a witch doctor. He gave her some leaves as medication, and told them she would be better. She didn't get better, but she got worse.

Although she was only eight, her health began to spiral down. Her parents were not Christians. There was not even a Christian church in the village.

When her parents realized she was becoming sicker, they took her to another witch doctor. They were told that the sickness wasn't a medical problem, but rather a curse that someone had put on her. (This is a witch doctor's usual diagnosis.) Missoule's parents became more indebted to the witch doctors, while their daughter became sicker. Finally, they resorted to medical doctors; but they, as well, could not find the cause of her illness.

Because she was so sick, she was frequently absent from school. Concentrating on books and lessons became more difficult.

In the course of eight years, she was taken to 21 different witch doctors and many physicians. Yet, none of them had any answers. Sometimes she would be paralyzed. After a few days, the paralysis would leave. Then she would be blind, or intense pain would wrack her body. The cycle repeated itself many times during those years. This strange sickness had no known cure.

When her parents would tell her they were taking her to another witch doctor, she would protest and cry. She had little power to resist her parents' demands. She feared what the doctor would do to her. Her condition did not improve.

Ten years later, when Missoule was eighteen, missionaries came to her village. They shared the Gospel with the whole village, and planted a church there. Missoule's mother gave her life to the Lord, and her father accepted the Lord five years later.

One day, Missoule became very ill, near death. She appeared to be in a coma. She heard people crying for her. She heard them saying they would go for a casket.

In the midst of those mourning around her bed, Missoule felt herself ascending a very high hill, where everything was beautiful and peaceful. When she reached the top of the hill, she met a tall man dressed in white. She was very excited to be there, away from her pain. Then the man told her "You must return to where you came from."

"No. Please let me stay. I don't want to return," she begged. She turned her head, and saw many vicious dogs, baring their teeth.

Again the man said, "Return. There is work to do. I am not ready for you yet."

Trembling, she started down the hill. People from the church were there praying for her when she woke up. That day she gave her heart to the Lord. She was healed immediately. She never experienced paralysis or blindness after that.

Later, Missoule's aunt told her, "I am so sorry for what I have done."

"What do you mean, Auntie?" she asked.

"When you were a little girl and in school, I had a curse put on you," her aunt said.

"But why?" Missoule asked.

"You did so well in school, and so much better than my own children, I was very jealous. I wanted to harm you," she explained.

"But now, I cannot take the curse away. I destroyed the voodoo elements I used for the curse. I can't reverse the curse. I am so sorry," she said.

Missoule listened intently, and then said "Auntie, the curse has been lifted. God took it away. He didn't need the elements. God is more powerful than a curse."

"But God will redeem my soul from the power of the grave, For He shall receive me. Selah" —Psalm 49:15

FIRE! FIRE!

"You will keep him in perfect peace, Whose mind is stayed on You, Because he trusts in You." Isaiah 26:3

"Fire, fire!! Please open the door!!" Someone was banging on our bedroom door, trying to wake us. It was five-thirty in the morning.

We had heard the screams, but thought it was someone in the street causing a ruckus. The banging on the door continued. Finally, jolted from sleep, we jumped from bed. As we opened the door, we were blinded by intense smoke.

Our house was on fire! Smoke had already filled the entire second story. We could not tell where the fire was coming from. The children were still sleeping. Agape was on our end of the house, but Rachel's room was on the other side of the family room.

I feared for Agape, as he had many allergies. Smoke of this intensity would certainly be tragic for him. Entering his room in haste, I was shocked. He was sound asleep on his stomach. The smoke was dense, but a space above him the length of the bed was clear of any smoke. God had sent an angel of protection to watch over him. I grabbed him and ran to the other side of the house to Rachel's room. She was also sound asleep, not knowing we were in danger.

We ran downstairs blindly and forced the door open to leave the house. Neighbors were already throwing buckets of water toward the flames which were coming from the kitchen windows. Someone called the fire trucks and the response was, "We cannot come; there's no fuel in the truck." Humor can be found in most situations.

After the flames finally died down, we entered the house. Then we realized the cause of the fire. When the electrical power had been turned on early that morning by the city, the surge coming into the house was so strong that it set the refrigerator on fire. It had melted down to a lump of metal. Although the house was smoke damaged, no one was hurt or burned.

For many years I kept the charred cookbooks and the partially-melted recipe box as a reminder of God's protection and grace during a very stressful time. I never threw them away, but they were destroyed by the earthquake.

You know you have lived in Haiti when...

you take a bath in the canal and a cow nearby
turns it's head.

IDOL OR SAINT?

"You shall have no other gods before me." Exodus 20:3

His grandmother taught Patrick the ways of the Catholic Church, and the importance of praying to Mother Mary. She believed Mother Mary had power, and could help Patrick in school.

Following his grandma's advice, he went to church every morning on his way to school, asking Mother Mary to help him with his lessons and exams, but got confused. Mary never helped. Nothing changed. His lessons were difficult, and exams did not become easier.

The older he got the more he grew away from the church. Then he remembered a story his grandma had told him when he was a young boy.

"My dear one, I will tell you a special story that happened when I was a young girl." His grandma began.

"Every year there was a celebration for the Catholic patron saint for each village. Our patron saint was St. Louis. People came from many villages for this great event. The celebration started with mass at the church, and then the large statue of St. Louis was carried at the front of a parade as they marched through the town.

"One time, as the leaders were carrying St. Louis down the church steps something terrible happened. The statue got off imbalance and fell to the ground. It broke in a thousand pieces. The rest of the celebration was not so joyful."

This story lay dormant in Patrick's heart for many years. Then one day he said, "Grandma, I will no longer be attending the church."

"Patrick, you cannot dismiss the church and the mass, praying to the Saints and Mary," she said, angrily.

"The saints are nothing but rocks, and Mary can't help anyone," Patrick replied.

"Oh my, oh my! God help my son! What has happened to him?" she cried.

"Grandma, you told me the saints were rocks. Remember the story about St. Louis? You told me he fell and broke. If he was real and had power, he could have repaired himself. But he didn't. I cannot pray to rocks anymore," Patrick explained.

Grandma could not be consoled. She was convinced that Patrick would be lost forever. But years later, he found the One who could hear and answer his prayers.

THE POWER OF PRAYER

"Pray without ceasing." I Thessalonians 5:17

Thomas was raised by his father, who always wanted to protect his two sons. Because of the Christian influence in the home, Thomas learned to love and trust Jesus at a very young age. When Thomas was nine years old, he was baptized. He continued to grow in his walk with the Lord. Thomas also learned to be very cautious, especially when it came to trusting people.

"Boys," said his father, "Elda, my cousin, would like you to come for a visit."

The boys left, but instead of going to Elda's they went to Robert's home, a church leader, and had been there a while when their father appeared.

"Boys," he said sternly, "I told you to go to Elda's house. What are you doing here?"

"I'm sorry, Dad," Thomas replied, "but you know Elda is a witch doctor. I don't want to see her."

Thomas looked at Robert, and Robert agreed, "Joe,

you know what Elda is. The boys are young. They do not need her influence."

Several years later he married Margaret, a wonderful Christian girl. After several years of marriage, they received wonderful news. They were going to have a baby.

Margaret had a good pregnancy, but nine months passed, and the baby has not been born. At ten months, she still had no signs of labor.

One night toward the end of the tenth month, Thomas realized that her condition was not good, and that she would probably lose the baby. The baby did not seem to be moving anymore.

He prayed, asking for direction. At ten o'clock that night, he began to pray for Margaret. She was sleeping soundly. He simply went and put his hand above her abdomen, not touching her. He prayed silently, so as not to wake her. "God spare our baby, and bring life to it again. Heal my wife and give her strength," he prayed.

After praying, he went to the other bed in the same room and lay down. He felt peace, yet he had no visible answer to his prayer.

At midnight, he heard Margaret turn in her bed. He waited.

"Thomas," she called softly. He didn't answer.

Again, she called, "Thomas." He didn't answer.

Then on the third call, he replied, "Yes, my dear one, what is it?"

"Oh, my stomach," she cried, "I think the baby is coming."

She was in labor. He watched and waited. At three o'clock in the morning, a healthy baby was born. Thomas and Margaret knew that God had healed and brought life to their baby.

A THOUSAND SHALL FALL

"A thousand shall fall at thy side, and ten thousand at thy right hand; but it shall not come nigh thee."
—Psalm 91:7

"You should read Psalm 91," Pierre heard the still, small voice that morning. He had gone to Port-au-Prince, and would be leaving soon to return home. He quickly took his Bible and read the Psalm, not understanding why he felt he should read it.

When he arrived at the bus station, people were everywhere, pushing and shoving to get on a truck or bus that would take them to their destinations.

Pierre boarded a bus, but it had no vacant seats. He tried another one, but the answer was the same: "There are no seats left." After several more tries, he resorted to a truck that was filling up quickly, even though it had no seats. There was standing room only, with a rope to hang on to. This was his last chance to get home that day, so he jumped on the truck and hung on.

The truck was speeding along on the south highway, out of the city. After several hours of travel, the truck started the climb up the mountain. Pierre had fallen asleep, while standing and hanging on to the rope.

"Hey, look at that bus coming down the mountain!! It is racing at full speed!" Pierre heard it in his sleep, but did not grasp what was being said.

"The bus is coming straight toward us, not slowing down." He was still asleep, standing up.

Then there was a crash, and all was totally silent. Pierre wasn't sure where he was, or what had happened. He felt he was underneath a building. But as he tried to lift his head, he felt a vehicle moving over him.

Quickly putting his head down, he lay very still as the vehicle passed over him. Finally when he felt it was safe, he turned his head to one side. What he saw was terrifying. Bodies were lying everywhere. He slowly turned his head to the other side, and saw pools of blood and more bodies.

Immediately he remembered what he had read that morning in the Bible.

Soon He lifted his head higher, then eased himself up, and finally sat up. He remembered his friend who was traveling with him. He looked everywhere but couldn't find her. Finally, he saw her, lying with open arms to one side of the highway.

Quickly he ran to her. She didn't seem to be alive. He grabbed her and carried her to the highway. Gently laying her down, he pounded on her chest and breathed into her mouth. He waited. Then he repeated his actions. Finally, she began to breathe, looked up at him, and asked, "What happened? Where are we?"

He told her, "What I understand is that a bus came down the mountain with no brakes. I really don't know how it all happened, but I do know God is with us. He spared our lives, just as He promised me this morning."

You know you have lived in Haiti when...

Chickens, goats and people ride on the same bus into the city.

AN IMPORTANT INVITATION

"For as the heavens are higher than the earth, So are My ways higher than your ways, And My thoughts than your thoughts." —Isaiah 55:9

"Hello, Denis? It's Patrick. Hey, I want to invite you to the upcoming Bible School. I think you'll enjoy it."

"Well, thanks, but I think I'll pass. I've already been to another one. But thanks for the invitation," Denis said.

After some time had passed, Denis' phone rang again. "Hello, Denis? This is Patrick. I just thought I'd check in to see if you had changed your mind about attending Bible School."

"Well, I really don't think so," replied Denis.

Several weeks later Denis received another call. "Denis" Patrick said, "I really think you should try Bible School. I wish you would reconsider."

Denis thought for a minute and said, "Okay, so maybe I should. Let me know when classes are starting. I'll be there."

But when he went he thought this is useless. He already knew all there was to know about the Bible—or so he thought. When it was time for homework, he realized he couldn't even begin to do the lessons. It was so much more complex than he had ever imagined it would be.

He saw that the only thing left to do was to discard his "know-it-all" attitude, humble himself, and start the learning process all over again. Soon he loved the class and realized he was exactly where God wanted him.

He was convinced of this, and one day when he received a call from his family he knew it was true. "Denis," his brother Luke said, "I have bad news and don't even want to tell you."

"What happened?" Denis asked anxiously.

"Our brother, Philippe, isn't with us anymore."

"What? What happened?" Denis asked

"Last night there was a lightning storm in the village. Philippe was on the porch, as he always is in the evening. He had his radio on his lap, listening to the news. Then lightning struck the radio and killed him instantly."

As Denis thought about this situation, he knew God had protected him. He lived next door to Philippe. They always sat on the porch together, listening to the news. He too, would have been struck by the lightning had he not been at Bible School.

Denis is now a pastor in one of the villages.

SARAH'S STORY

"Behold, I stand at the door and knock. If anyone hears My voice and opens the door, I will come in to him and dine with him, and he with Me."
—Revelation 3:20

Walking across the rocky, dusty ground toward the church, I met Sarah, standing alone. Putting my arm around her thin body, I said, "Sarah, come, let's sit and talk."

Her face lit up, with her million-dollar smile. She always had a smile for everyone, especially when she was in church.

We entered the new church building, found an empty wooden bench in the back, and sat down.

"Sarah, talk to me. Tell me a good story about your life, and how God has blessed it."

Sarah smiled, her dark eyes were sparkling. She clasped her hands together, and started her story.

"My parents were not Christians, so it was difficult for them to be a good example to me. They weren't exactly in voodoo, but did visit the witch doctor's place at times, especially when we were sick.

"We were raised Catholic, which was all they knew. The day-by-day struggles never became easier. Life was quite mundane, without hope.

"One day my younger brother got sick, and was in bed for many, many days. We had no hope for his recovery. Each day we prayed to Mother Mary and all the Saints. Nothing happened. We continued our prayers with no results. Then a Christian lady came to our house. When she heard how we prayed, she said, "You are praying to the wrong god. You need to pray to the only God and not the saints and Mary."

"When we prayed to God my brother was healed.

"Then I started to change my life, and tried to live a Christian life. But it didn't last long. Soon I was involved in various aspects of voodoo, trying to kill people and sending curses on others. I don't even like to tell people what my life was like before Jesus.

"Then a man arrived at my door. Thinking this was the answer to my miserable life, I started a relationship with him. Soon I became pregnant; then he left. I didn't see him for a long time. My first son was born. Soon after that, my boyfriend came back. Once again, I became pregnant.

"I was disgusted with life, but I didn't know where to turn for help. I moved to another village, one that had a Protestant church. When my second son was born, I stayed in this village, and started attending the church.

God touched my heart, and I made the decision to live for Jesus.

"Now I am married to a Christian man, and we have a family together. Although life has not been easy, and we have suffered a lot, I would not exchange my life with Jesus for anything here on earth. God is my best friend. He takes care of me. I love Him very much."

God has given Sarah a new life in Him.

THE PROFESSOR

"Because the foolishness of God is wiser than men, and the weakness of God is stronger than men." I Corinthians 1:25

Patrick was invited to be the guest speaker at a local church in Port-au-Prince. The church was filled—standing room only. As he stepped to the podium, he looked out over the crowd and recognized a man who he'd not seen for many years.

Patrick had attended high school in Jeremie, his home town. This man had been his literature professor.

Before Patrick started preaching, he said, "I would like to acknowledge someone here in the crowd."

Looking at the man, he said, "Sir, I must thank you tonight for being my teacher. I appreciate the time you invested in me while I was in your class. You taught me well, and you were an integral part of my preparation to be where I am tonight."

Then he started preaching. His text was in I Corinthians 1:25. He explained how foolish it is to think our education will make us wise before God.

After preaching, he took his seat. Patrick had a surprise awaiting him.

The professor stood and asked permission to speak. "Tonight I see that my student has become my professor. I have been an atheist all my life. I have been searching for the truth. I was very proud of my education. I thought I was a wise man. But my wisdom didn't satisfy my heart. Tonight I have found true Wisdom, and I want to give my life to God."

FROM TRAGEDY TO TRIUMPH

"Yet in all these things we are more than conquerors through Him who loved us." Romans 8:37

Life is a new normal since the earthquake. Most of Haiti still lays in ruins. There are thousands of people living in tent camps. They are hoping for deliverance from their despicable life. Rape, disease and robbery are a constant threat. The Haiti we knew will be no more.

We lost much—our home and all its contents, the mission compound, and an arm and a leg. I had teacups from my children and many friends. In that collection, I had a small cup that had been given to my father from his aunt more than 60 years ago. I had a special quilt from my grandmother and a quilt from my mother. I had no choice which one of these treasures I should give up. It has felt as if we have lost our freedom. We've had to depend on others to take us to the doctor, the store and church. We don't have a vehicle yet, or have a own home of our own. I don't say all this as a complaint, but to help you understand the effects of a tragedy. God tells us not to worry about what we will eat or wear, and in our case, where we will live.

Someone said to me, "You make this all look so easy." But it isn't easy. It isn't easy to depend on others for the simple things in life. It isn't easy to see our fellow missionaries continue their work in Haiti, and we are not in Haiti. Our hearts stay in Haiti. Haiti needs those missionaries.

We know that God didn't answer Patrick's prayer to take him home because He still has work for him to do. He has already had an opportunity to share the Gospel with several fellow amputees.

The work will continue. While Patrick was under the rubble, he felt a stronger burden not only to continue the work in Haiti, but also to expand it to the Haitians in the US. Our vision is to clone what we have done in Haiti—teach the Bible, train leaders and plant churches. Our prayer is that Haitians in the US will have a vision and burden to be missionaries back to Haiti. We also want to provide other resources—teaching English, offer course for preparation for their GED diploma, and helping them to learn a vocation.

Above all, our ultimate goal is to bring glory to God, the One who sent His son to die for us. Jesus is our Conqueror in every battle. As we follow Him, we look forward to the final triumph He has already won for us!

CPSIA information can be obtained at www.ICGtesting.com
Printed in the USA
LVOW071000190911

246856LV00001B/1/P